GLOBETROTTER™

*Travel Atlas*

# SOUTH AFRICA

NEW
HOLLAND

New Holland Publishers (UK) Ltd
London • Cape Town • Sydney • Auckland

First edition        1994
Second impression    1995
Third impression     1996
Fourth impression    1997
Second edition       1997
Second impression    1998
Third impression     2000
Third edition        2001
Fourth edition       2003
Fifth edition        2005
Sixth edition        2006
Seventh edition      2009

10 9 8 7 6 5 4 3 2 1

website: www.newhollandpublishers.com

Garfield House, 86 Edgware Road
London W2 2EA
United Kingdom

80 McKenzie Street
Cape Town 8001
South Africa

Unit 1, 66 Gibbes Street
Chatswood NSW 2067
Australia

218 Lake Road
Northcote, Auckland
New Zealand

Distributed in the USA by
The Globe Pequot Press, Connecticut

ISBN 978 1 84773 354 2

**Publishing Manager:** Thea Grobbelaar
**DTP Cartographic Manager:** Genené Hart
**Editors:** Carla Zietsman, Alicha van Reenen, Melany McCallum,
Tarryn Berry
**Designer:** Nicole Bannister
**Cartographers:** Nicole Bannister, Genené Hart
**Compiler/Verifier:** Denielle Lategan, Elaine Fick

Reproduction by Hirt & Carter, Cape Town
Printed and bound by Times Offset (M) Sdn. Bhd., Malaysia.

**Cover:** *Scenic view of False Bay, Cape Town.*
**Title Page:** *The Wilderness coastline, part of the well-known
Garden Route.*

**Photographic Credits:**
Herman Potgieter, page 33; IOA/Shaen Adey,
pages 49, 59; IOA/CLB, page 24; IOA/Roger de la
Harpe, pages 30, 67; IOA/Gerhard Dreyer, title
page, page 40; IOA/Walter Knirr, pages 10, 16,
18, 54, 70 (bottom), 72, 80; IOA/Peter Pickford,
page 74; IOA/Erhardt Thiel, pages 46, 48, 50;
IOA/Hein von Hörsten, cover, pages 35, 39, 62;
IOA/Lanz von Hörsten, pages 20, 42, 45, 78;
IOA/Keith Young, pages 26, 28, 57, 61, 70 (top).
*[IOA: Images of Africa; CLB: Colour Library]*

This atlas has been written by independent authors
and updaters. The information therein represents their
impartial opinion, and neither they nor the publishers
accept payment in return for including in the book or
writing more favourable reviews of any of the estab-
lishments. Whilst every effort has been made to
ensure that this guidebook is as accurate and up to
date as possible, please be aware that the facts quot-
ed are subject to change, particularly the price of
food, transport and accommodation. The Publisher
accepts no responsibility or liability for any loss, injury
or inconvenience incurred by readers or travellers
using this atlas.

## Emergency Telephone Numbers
## Notrufnummern
## Appels d'Urgence

| | |
|---|---|
| Police | |
| Polizeirevier | 1-0111 |
| Poste de police | |
| | |
| Telephone enquiries | |
| Telefon Auskunft | 1-023 |
| Information téléphonique | |
| | |
| Ambulance | |
| Krankenwagen | 1-0177 |
| Ambulances | |

**Below:** *This brightly coloured South African flag was
first raised at midnight on 26 April 1994. For most South
Africans it is a symbol of hope, uniting the nation in its
effort to reconciliate and become a truly democratic
society.*

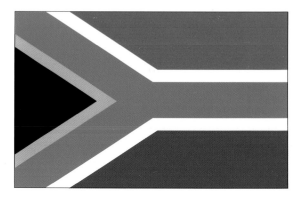

# CONTENTS

## TOURIST AREAS

## MAIN MAP SECTION

## INDEX

For ease of use, the Index has been divided into two sections:

• the first focuses on the Tourist Area Maps and related text and photographs.

• the second deals with the Main Map Section only, facilitating the easy location of cities, towns and villages.

# National Route Planner

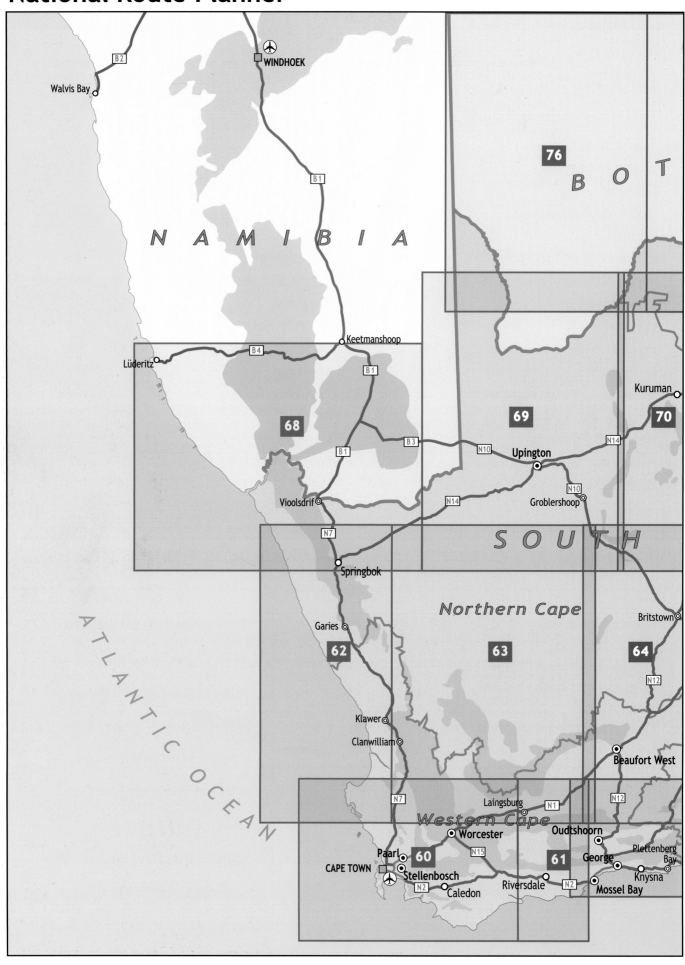

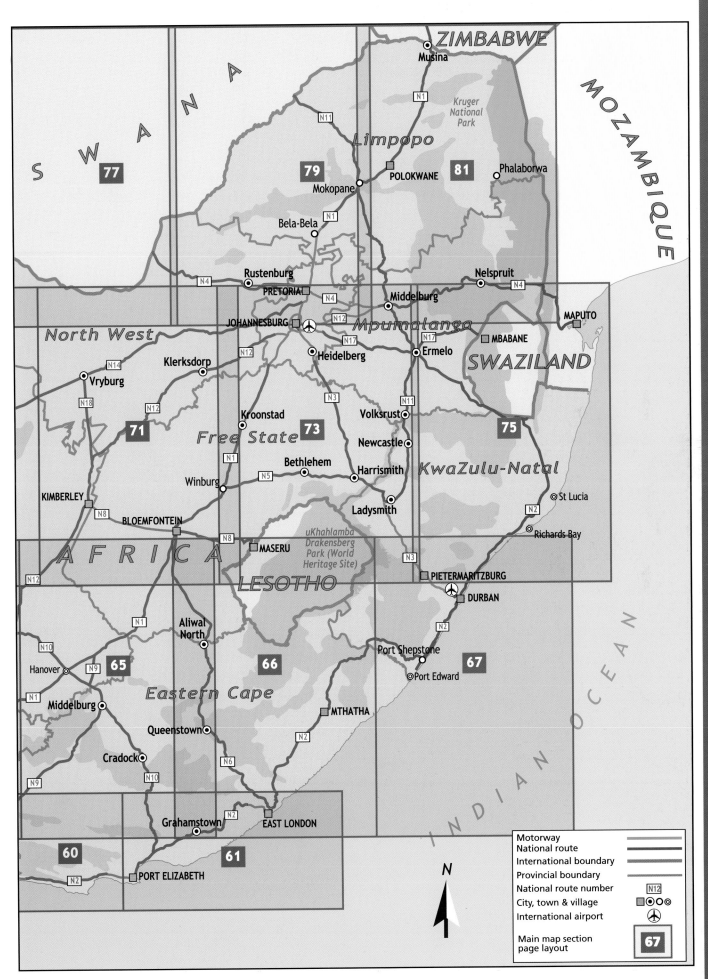

**Legend**

| | |
|---|---|
| Motorway | |
| National route | |
| International boundary | |
| Provincial boundary | |
| National route number | N12 |
| City, town & village | ◼ ⊙ ◎ |
| International airport | ✈ |
| Main map section page layout | 67 |

# Tourist Area Planner

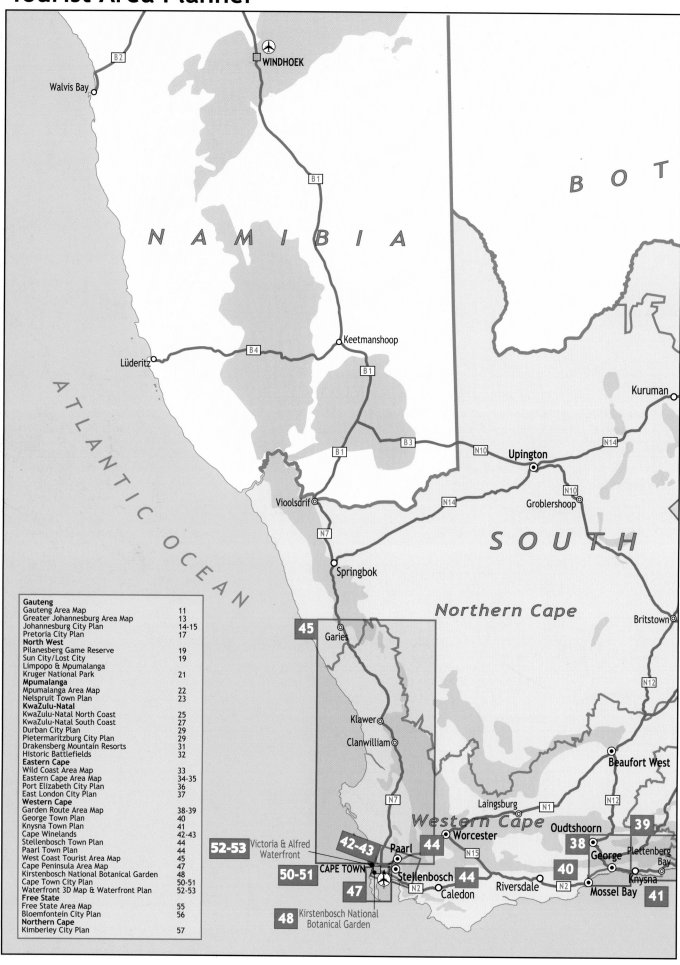

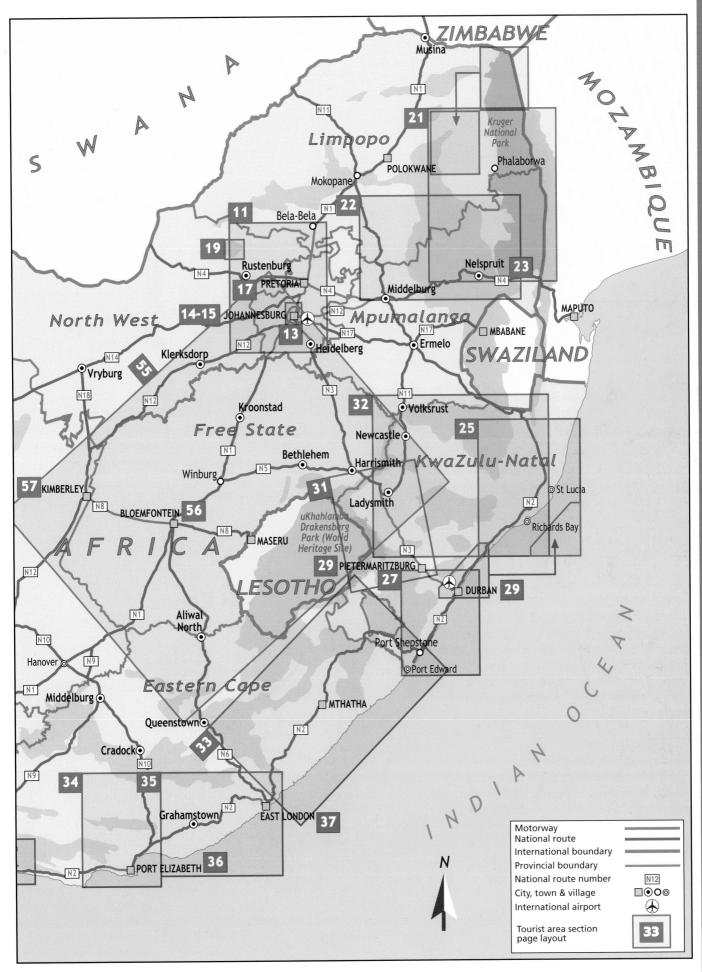

# Distance Chart

| APPROXIMATE DISTANCES IN KILOMETRES | BLOEMFONTEIN | CAPE TOWN | DURBAN | EAST LONDON | GABORONE | GRAHAMSTOWN | JOHANNESBURG | KIMBERLEY | MAPUTO | MASERU | MBABANE | PORT ELIZABETH | PRETORIA | WELKOM | WINDHOEK |
|---|---|---|---|---|---|---|---|---|---|---|---|---|---|---|---|
| BEAUFORT WEST | 544 | 460 | 1178 | 605 | 1042 | 492 | 942 | 504 | 1349 | 609 | 1129 | 501 | 1000 | 697 | 1629 |
| BLOEMFONTEIN | | 1004 | 634 | 584 | 622 | 601 | 398 | 177 | 897 | 157 | 677 | 677 | 456 | 153 | 1593 |
| BRITSTOWN | 398 | 710 | 1032 | 609 | 791 | 496 | 725 | 253 | 1289 | 555 | 1075 | 572 | 783 | 551 | 1378 |
| CAPE TOWN | 1004 | | 1753 | 1099 | 1501 | 899 | 1402 | 962 | 1900 | 1160 | 1680 | 769 | 1460 | 1156 | 1500 |
| COLESBERG | 226 | 778 | 860 | 488 | 848 | 375 | 624 | 292 | 1123 | 383 | 903 | 451 | 682 | 379 | 1573 |
| DE AAR | 346 | 762 | 980 | 557 | 843 | 444 | 744 | 305 | 1243 | 503 | 1023 | 520 | 802 | 499 | 1430 |
| DURBAN | 634 | 1753 | | 674 | 979 | 864 | 578 | 811 | 625 | 590 | 562 | 984 | 646 | 564 | 2227 |
| EAST LONDON | 584 | 1079 | 674 | | 1206 | 180 | 982 | 780 | 1301 | 630 | 1238 | 310 | 1040 | 737 | 1987 |
| GABORONE | 622 | 1501 | 979 | 1206 | | 1223 | 358 | 538 | 957 | 702 | 719 | 1299 | 350 | 479 | 1735 |
| GEORGE | 773 | 438 | 1319 | 645 | 1361 | 465 | 1171 | 762 | 1670 | 913 | 1450 | 335 | 1229 | 926 | 1887 |
| GRAAFF-REINET | 424 | 787 | 942 | 395 | 1012 | 282 | 822 | 490 | 1321 | 599 | 1101 | 291 | 880 | 577 | 1697 |
| GRAHAMSTOWN | 601 | 899 | 854 | 180 | 1223 | | 999 | 667 | 1478 | 692 | 1418 | 130 | 1057 | 754 | 1856 |
| HARRISMITH | 328 | 1331 | 306 | 822 | 673 | 929 | 282 | 505 | 649 | 284 | 468 | 1068 | 332 | 258 | 1921 |
| JOHANNESBURG | 398 | 1402 | 578 | 982 | 358 | 999 | | 472 | 599 | 438 | 361 | 1075 | 58 | 258 | 1801 |
| KEETMANSHOOP | 1088 | 995 | 1722 | 1482 | 1230 | 1351 | 1296 | 911 | 1895 | 1245 | 1657 | 1445 | 1354 | 1205 | 505 |
| KIMBERLEY | 177 | 962 | 811 | 780 | 538 | 667 | 472 | | 1071 | 334 | 833 | 743 | 530 | 294 | 1416 |
| KLERKSDORP | 288 | 1271 | 645 | 872 | 334 | 889 | 164 | 308 | 763 | 368 | 525 | 1009 | 222 | 145 | 1693 |
| KROONSTAD | 211 | 1214 | 537 | 795 | 442 | 812 | 187 | 339 | 742 | 247 | 522 | 888 | 245 | 71 | 1724 |
| LADYSMITH | 410 | 1413 | 236 | 752 | 755 | 932 | 356 | 587 | 567 | 366 | 386 | 1062 | 422 | 340 | 2008 |
| MAFIKENG | 464 | 1343 | 821 | 1048 | 158 | 1065 | 287 | 380 | 886 | 544 | 648 | 1141 | 294 | 321 | 1577 |
| MAPUTO | 897 | 1900 | 625 | 1301 | 957 | 1478 | 599 | 1071 | | 853 | 223 | 1609 | 583 | 813 | 2400 |
| MASERU | 157 | 1160 | 590 | 630 | 702 | 692 | 438 | 334 | 853 | | 633 | 822 | 488 | 249 | 1750 |
| MBABANE | 677 | 1680 | 562 | 1238 | 719 | 1418 | 361 | 833 | 223 | 633 | | 1548 | 372 | 451 | 2162 |
| MTHATHA | 570 | 1314 | 439 | 235 | 1192 | 415 | 869 | 747 | 1064 | 616 | 1003 | 545 | 928 | 718 | 2066 |
| MUSINA | 928 | 1932 | 1118 | 1512 | 696 | 1529 | 530 | 1002 | 725 | 960 | 808 | 1605 | 472 | 788 | 2331 |
| NELSPRUIT | 757 | 1762 | 707 | 1226 | 672 | 1358 | 355 | 827 | 244 | 713 | 173 | 1434 | 322 | 639 | 2156 |
| OUDTSHOORN | 743 | 506 | 1294 | 704 | 1241 | 532 | 1141 | 703 | 1705 | 959 | 1417 | 394 | 1199 | 896 | 1828 |
| PIETERMARITZBURG | 555 | 1674 | 79 | 595 | 900 | 775 | 509 | 732 | 706 | 511 | 640 | 905 | 567 | 485 | 2148 |
| POLOKWANE | 717 | 1721 | 907 | 1301 | 485 | 1318 | 319 | 791 | 605 | 749 | 515 | | 261 | 577 | 2120 |
| PORT ELIZABETH | 677 | 769 | 984 | 310 | 1299 | 130 | 1075 | 743 | 1609 | 822 | 1548 | | 1394 | 830 | 1950 |
| PRETORIA | 456 | 1460 | 646 | 1040 | 350 | 1057 | 58 | 530 | 583 | 488 | 372 | 1133 | | 316 | 1859 |
| QUEENSTOWN | 377 | 1069 | 676 | 207 | 999 | 269 | 775 | 554 | 1302 | 423 | 1240 | 399 | 833 | 525 | 1829 |
| UPINGTON | 588 | 894 | 1222 | 982 | 730 | 851 | 796 | 411 | 1395 | 745 | 1157 | 945 | 854 | 669 | 1005 |
| WELKOM | 153 | 1156 | 564 | 737 | 479 | 754 | 258 | 294 | 813 | 249 | 451 | 830 | 316 | | 1679 |
| WINDHOEK | 1593 | 1500 | 2227 | 1987 | 1735 | 1856 | 1801 | 1416 | 2400 | 1750 | 2162 | 1950 | 1859 | 1679 | |

# Strip Route

## Strip Routes

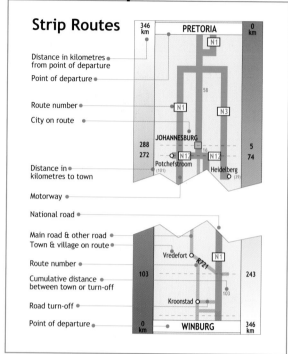

## Strip Routes

Strip routes are located throughout the atlas to indicate the distances between major centres in a specific region. Distances between other towns and villages along the route are also shown.

## Distance Charts

In order to calculate the distance between two of the country's major centres, locate the name of the first town or city on the vertical or horizontal column on the chart (see above), then locate the name of the other on the second column and read off the number where the vertical and horizontal columns intersect.

## Toll Road Chart

Various South African provinces are served by time-saving toll roads. The chart (right) identifies the names of these toll roads, the locations of the toll plazas, points between which the toll roads stretch, and grid references for locating these roads on the maps in this book.

# Toll Roads

| ROUTE | PROVINCE | NAME | TOLL PLAZA | LOCATION |
|---|---|---|---|---|
| N1 | Western Cape | HUGUENOT TUNNEL | HUGUENOT | DU TOITSKLOOF |
| N1 | Free State | KROONVAAL | VAAL | UNCLE CHARLIES-KROONSTAD |
| N1 | Gauteng | | GRASMERE | JHB-VANDERBIJLPARK |
| N1 | Limpopo | KRANSKOP | KRANSKOP | BELA-BELA-MIDDELFONTEIN |
| N2 | Western Cape | TSITSIKAMMA | TSITSIKAMMA | THE CRAGS AND STORMS RIVER |
| N2 | KwaZulu-Natal | SOUTH COAST | ORIBI | SOUTHBROOM-MARBURG |
| N2 | KwaZulu-Natal | | IZOTSHA | SOUTHBROOM-MARBURG |
| N2 | KwaZulu-Natal | NORTH COAST | TONGAAT | UMDLOTI-BALLITO |
| N2 | KwaZulu-Natal | | UMVOTI | SHAKASKRAAL/STANGER |
| N2 | KwaZulu-Natal | | MTUNZINI | MTUNZINI/FELIXTON |
| N3 | Free State | HIGHVELD | WILGE | VILLIERS-WARDEN |
| N3 | KwaZulu-Natal | MIDLANDS | TUGELA | KEEVERSFONTEIN-FRERE |
| N3 | KwaZulu-Natal | | MOOI RIVER | FRERE-CEDARA |
| N3 | KwaZulu-Natal | MARIANNHILL | MARIANNHILL | ASSAGAY-PINETOWN |
| N4 | Gauteng | MAGALIES | QUAGGA | PRETORIA-ATTERIDGEVILLE |
| N4 | Gauteng | | PELINDABA | ATTERIDGEVILLE-PELINDABA |
| N17 | Gauteng | WITWATERSRAND | DALPARK | SPRINGS-DALPARK |
| N17 | Gauteng | | DENNE ROAD | SPRINGS-DALPARK |
| N17 | Gauteng | | GOSFORTH | DALPARK-RAND AIRPORT |

# Climate Chart

## Climate Charts

These occur throughout the atlas, and give the average temperatures and rainfall for the relevant region or city.

| JOHANNESBURG | J | F | M | A | M | J | J | A | S | O | N | D |
|---|---|---|---|---|---|---|---|---|---|---|---|---|
| AV. TEMP. °C | 20 | 20 | 18 | 16 | 13 | 10 | 10 | 13 | 16 | 18 | 18 | 19 |
| AV. TEMP. °F | 68 | 68 | 64 | 61 | 55 | 50 | 50 | 55 | 61 | 64 | 64 | 66 |
| DAILY SUN hrs | 8 | 8 | 8 | 9 | 9 | 9 | 9 | 10 | 9 | 9 | 8 | 8 |
| RAINFALL mm | 131 | 95 | 81 | 55 | 19 | 7 | 6 | 6 | 26 | 72 | 114 | 106 |
| RAINFALL in | 5.5 | 4 | 3.5 | 2.5 | 0.7 | 0.3 | 0.2 | 0.2 | 1 | 3 | 4.5 | 4.5 |

| PRETORIA | J | F | M | A | M | J | J | A | S | O | N | D |
|---|---|---|---|---|---|---|---|---|---|---|---|---|
| AV. TEMP. °C | 23 | 22 | 21 | 18 | 15 | 11 | 12 | 14 | 18 | 20 | 21 | 22 |
| AV. TEMP. °F | 73 | 72 | 70 | 64 | 59 | 52 | 54 | 57 | 64 | 68 | 70 | 73 |
| DAILY SUN hrs | 9 | 8 | 8 | 8 | 9 | 9 | 9 | 10 | 10 | 9 | 9 | 9 |
| RAINFALL mm | 152 | 76 | 80 | 57 | 14 | 3 | 3 | 6 | 21 | 67 | 101 | 105 |
| RAINFALL in | 6 | 3 | 3.5 | 2.5 | 0.6 | 0.1 | 0.1 | 0.2 | 0.8 | 3 | 4 | 4.5 |

| BLOEMFONTEIN | J | F | M | A | M | J | J | A | S | O | N | D |
|---|---|---|---|---|---|---|---|---|---|---|---|---|
| AV. TEMP. °C | 23 | 21 | 19 | 15 | 11 | 7 | 7 | 10 | 14 | 17 | 19 | 22 |
| AV. TEMP. °F | 73 | 70 | 66 | 59 | 52 | 45 | 45 | 50 | 57 | 63 | 66 | 72 |
| DAILY SUN hrs | 10 | 9 | 9 | 9 | 9 | 9 | 9 | 9 | 10 | 10 | 10 | 10 |
| RAINFALL mm | 91 | 99 | 74 | 58 | 21 | 12 | 9 | 14 | 19 | 42 | 59 | 62 |
| RAINFALL in | 4 | 4 | 3 | 2.5 | 0.8 | 0.5 | 0.3 | 0.6 | 0.7 | 2 | 2.5 | 2.5 |

| DURBAN | J | F | M | A | M | J | J | A | S | O | N | D |
|---|---|---|---|---|---|---|---|---|---|---|---|---|
| AV. TEMP. °C | 24 | 25 | 24 | 22 | 19 | 17 | 16 | 17 | 19 | 20 | 22 | 23 |
| AV. TEMP. °F | 75 | 77 | 75 | 72 | 66 | 63 | 61 | 63 | 66 | 68 | 72 | 73 |
| DAILY SUN hrs | 6 | 7 | 7 | 7 | 7 | 7 | 7 | 7 | 6 | 5 | 5 | 6 |
| RAINFALL mm | 135 | 114 | 124 | 87 | 64 | 26 | 44 | 58 | 65 | 89 | 104 | 108 |
| RAINFALL in | 5.5 | 4.5 | 5 | 3.5 | 3 | 1 | 2 | 2.5 | 3 | 4 | 4.5 | 4.5 |
| SEA TEMP. °C | 24 | 25 | 24 | 23 | 21 | 20 | 19 | 19 | 20 | 21 | 22 | 23 |
| SEA TEMP. °F | 75 | 77 | 75 | 73 | 70 | 68 | 66 | 66 | 68 | 70 | 72 | 73 |

| EAST LONDON | J | F | M | A | M | J | J | A | S | O | N | D |
|---|---|---|---|---|---|---|---|---|---|---|---|---|
| AV. TEMP. °C | 22 | 22 | 21 | 19 | 18 | 16 | 16 | 16 | 17 | 18 | 19 | 21 |
| AV. TEMP. °F | 72 | 72 | 70 | 66 | 64 | 61 | 61 | 61 | 63 | 64 | 66 | 70 |
| DAILY SUN hrs | 7 | 7 | 7 | 7 | 7 | 7 | 8 | 7 | 7 | 7 | 7 | 8 |
| RAINFALL mm | 74 | 95 | 106 | 80 | 55 | 40 | 51 | 75 | 93 | 95 | 90 | 74 |
| RAINFALL in | 3 | 4 | 4.5 | 3.5 | 2.5 | 2 | 2.5 | 3 | 4 | 4 | 4 | 3.5 |
| SEA TEMP. °C | 19 | 19 | 18 | 18 | 17 | 17 | 17 | 17 | 17 | 18 | 18 | 18 |
| SEA TEMP. °F | 66 | 66 | 64 | 64 | 63 | 63 | 63 | 63 | 63 | 64 | 64 | 64 |

| PORT ELIZABETH | J | F | M | A | M | J | J | A | S | O | N | D |
|---|---|---|---|---|---|---|---|---|---|---|---|---|
| AV. TEMP. °C | 21 | 21 | 20 | 18 | 16 | 14 | 14 | 14 | 15 | 17 | 18 | 20 |
| AV. TEMP. °F | 70 | 70 | 68 | 64 | 61 | 57 | 57 | 57 | 59 | 63 | 64 | 68 |
| DAILY SUN hrs | 9 | 8 | 7 | 7 | 7 | 7 | 7 | 8 | 7 | 8 | 9 | 7 |
| RAINFALL mm | 41 | 39 | 55 | 57 | 68 | 61 | 54 | 75 | 70 | 59 | 49 | 34 |
| RAINFALL in | 2 | 2 | 2.5 | 2.5 | 3 | 2.5 | 2.5 | 3 | 3 | 2.5 | 2 | 1.5 |
| SEA TEMP. °C | 21 | 21 | 20 | 19 | 17 | 16 | 16 | 16 | 17 | 18 | 19 | 21 |
| SEA TEMP. °F | 70 | 70 | 68 | 66 | 63 | 61 | 61 | 61 | 63 | 64 | 66 | 70 |

| MOSSEL BAY | J | F | M | A | M | J | J | A | S | O | N | D |
|---|---|---|---|---|---|---|---|---|---|---|---|---|
| AV. TEMP. °C | 21 | 21 | 20 | 18 | 17 | 16 | 15 | 15 | 16 | 17 | 18 | 20 |
| AV. TEMP. °F | 70 | 70 | 68 | 64 | 63 | 61 | 59 | 59 | 61 | 63 | 64 | 68 |
| DAILY SUN hrs | 7 | 7 | 7 | 7 | 7 | 7 | 7 | 7 | 7 | 7 | 7 | 7 |
| RAINFALL mm | 28 | 31 | 36 | 40 | 37 | 31 | 32 | 36 | 39 | 38 | 34 | 28 |
| RAINFALL in | 1 | 1 | 1.5 | 2 | 1.5 | 1 | 1 | 1.5 | 2 | 1.5 | 1.5 | 1 |
| SEA TEMP. °C | 22 | 22 | 20 | 19 | 18 | 16 | 16 | 16 | 16 | 17 | 19 | 21 |
| SEA TEMP. °F | 72 | 72 | 68 | 66 | 64 | 61 | 61 | 61 | 61 | 63 | 66 | 70 |

| CAPE TOWN | J | F | M | A | M | J | J | A | S | O | N | D |
|---|---|---|---|---|---|---|---|---|---|---|---|---|
| AV. TEMP. °C | 21 | 21 | 20 | 17 | 15 | 13 | 12 | 13 | 14 | 16 | 18 | 20 |
| AV. TEMP. °F | 70 | 70 | 68 | 63 | 59 | 55 | 54 | 55 | 57 | 61 | 64 | 68 |
| DAILY SUN hrs | 11 | 10 | 9 | 7 | 6 | 6 | 6 | 7 | 8 | 9 | 10 | 11 |
| RAINFALL mm | 14 | 17 | 19 | 39 | 74 | 92 | 70 | 75 | 39 | 37 | 15 | 17 |
| RAINFALL in | 0.6 | 0.7 | 0.7 | 2 | 3 | 4 | 3 | 3 | 2 | 1.5 | 0.6 | 0.7 |
| SEA TEMP. °C | 15 | 15 | 14 | 13 | 13 | 12 | 12 | 13 | 13 | 13 | 14 | 14 |
| SEA TEMP. °F | 59 | 57 | 55 | 55 | 54 | 54 | 54 | 55 | 55 | 55 | 57 | 57 |

| LANGEBAAN | J | F | M | A | M | J | J | A | S | O | N | D |
|---|---|---|---|---|---|---|---|---|---|---|---|---|
| AV. TEMP. °C | 17 | 17 | 17 | 16 | 15 | 14 | 13 | 13 | 14 | 15 | 16 | 17 |
| AV. TEMP. °F | 63 | 63 | 63 | 61 | 59 | 57 | 55 | 55 | 57 | 59 | 61 | 63 |
| DAILY SUN hrs | 7 | 6 | 7 | 7 | 8 | 8 | 8 | 7 | 6 | 7 | 7 | 7 |
| RAINFALL mm | 3 | 2 | 6 | 15 | 20 | 21 | 22 | 18 | 11 | 8 | 4 | 5 |
| RAINFALL in | 0.1 | 0 | 0.2 | 0.6 | 0.8 | 0.8 | 0.9 | 0.7 | 0.4 | 0.3 | 0.1 | 0.2 |
| SEA TEMP. °C | 15 | 14 | 14 | 13 | 13 | 12 | 12 | 13 | 13 | 14 | 14 | 14 |
| SEA TEMP. °F | 59 | 57 | 57 | 55 | 55 | 54 | 54 | 54 | 55 | 55 | 57 | 57 |

# Legend

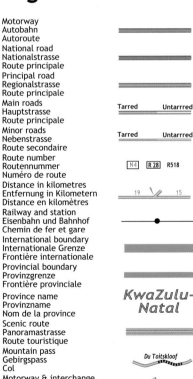

Motorway / Autobahn / Autoroute

National road / Nationalstrasse / Route principale

Principal road / Regionalstrasse / Route principale

Main roads / Hauptstrasse / Route principale — Tarred / Untarred

Minor roads / Nebenstrasse / Route secondaire — Tarred / Untarred

Route number / Routennummer / Numéro de route — N4   R28   R518

Distance in kilometres / Entfernung in Kilometern / Distance en kilomètres — 19   15

Railway and station / Eisenbahn und Bahnhof / Chemin de fer et gare

International boundary / Internationale Grenze / Frontière internationale

Provincial boundary / Provinzgrenze / Frontière provinciale

Province name / Provinzname / Nom de la province — *KwaZulu-Natal*

Scenic route / Panoramastrasse / Route touristique

Mountain pass / Gebirgspass / Col — *Du Toitskloof*

Motorway & interchange / Autobahn und -kreuz / Autoroute avec échangeur

National reserves and parks / Nationalreservat und Park / Réserve naturelle et parc — *Mountain Zebra NP*

Airport / Flughafen / Aéroport — INT. / Other

Golf course / Golfplatz / Terrain de golf

Major petrol stop / Grosse Tankstelle / Station-service

Place of interest / Sehenswürdigkeit / Endroit à visiter — ★ *Historic Houses*

Peak in metres / Höhe in Metern / Altitude (en mètres) — Table Mtn ▲ 1140 m

Mountain range / Gebirgskette / Chaîne de montagnes

Water / Gewässer / Eau — *River / Waterfall / Swamp / Dam*

Toll road / Mautstrasse / Route à péage — T

City / Gross-stadt / Grande ville — ■

Major town / Kreisstadt / Ville importante — ◉

Small town / Kleinstadt / Grand village — O

Large village / Grössere Ortschaft / Grand village — ◎

Village / Dorf / Village — o

Lighthouse / Leuchtturm / Phare

Border post / Grenzübergang / Frontière — Lebombo

Cave/Ruin / Höhle/Ruine / Grotte/Ruines

Hotel (selected) / Hotel (Auswahl) / Hôtel (sélectionné) — (H) ALBANY

Picnic site / Piekniekplatz / Pique nique

Safe bathing beach / Badestrand / Baignade autorisée

Viewpoint / Aussichtspunkt / Point de vue

Camp / Camp / Camp — ⌂

Battle site / Hist. Schlachtfeld / Lieu de bataille historique — ✕ *uLundi*

Caravan park / Wohnwagenpark / Camping pour caravanes

Motorway and slip road / Autobahn mit Zufahrtsstrasse / Autoroute et bretelle d'accès

Main road and mall / Haupt- und Einkaufsstrasse / Grand rue et rue piétonnière — MALL

Road / Strasse / Route

Built-up area / Wohngebiet / Agglomération

Building of Interest / Interessantes Bauwerke / Edifice intéressant — Kruger House

Museum / Museum / Museu — Agricultural Museum

College/University / Kollege/Universität / Collège/Université

School / Schule / École — Bergvlam High School

Church/Mosque / Kirche/Moschee / Église/Mosquée — △△

Shopping centre / Einkaufszentrum / Centre commercial — Ⓢ *The Workshop*

Information Centre / Auskunftsbüro / Centre d'information — ℹ

Parking area / Parkplatz / Parking — P

Library / Bibliothek / Bibliothèque

One-way street / Einbahnstrasse / Rue à sens-unique — →

Restaurant / Restaurant / Restaurant — Ⓡ

Post office / Postamt / Bureau de poste — ✉

Bus terminus / Busbahnhof / Terminus d'autobus

Police station / Polizeirevier / Poste de police — ●

Hospital / Krankenhaus / Hôpital — ⊕

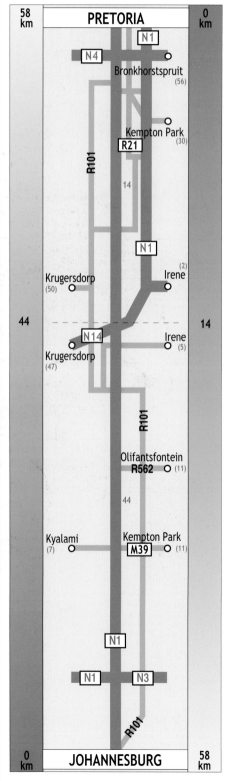

# Gauteng

*Johannesburg, bustling financial capital of Gauteng and South Africa's largest metropolis, and stately Pretoria, the country's administrative capital, are located 56km (35 miles) apart on the Highveld, the highest part of the great interior plateau. Southwest of central Johannesburg sprawls the urban conglomerate of Soweto, largest of the country's former 'African townships'; farther south is a concentration of industrial centres that includes Vereeniging and Vanderbijlpark, while to the north lie Johannesburg's affluent garden suburbs. All these form what is known as Gauteng — South Africa's pulsating economic heartland.*

## MAIN ATTRACTIONS

**Johannesburg:** South Africa's commercial and financial capital, a modern city dominated by concrete-and-glass giants (*see* page 12).
**Pretoria:** the lovely 'Jacaranda City' with a wealth of historic buildings; in October its avenues are strewn with lilac blossoms (*see* page 16).
**Sterkfontein Caves:** source of artefacts from the dawn of humankind, now a World Heritage Site.

**Hartbeespoort Dam:** picturesquely situated at the foothills of the Magaliesberg mountain range; popular with many anglers, campers and water-sports enthusiasts.
**Casino Entertainment complexes:** glittering venues, with much to offer besides gambling, include Sun City Resort and Casino Complex, Carnival City, Emperor's Palace, Montecasino, Gold Reef City and the Carousel.

## USEFUL CONTACTS

**Police,** tel: 1-0111 (national number).
**Ambulance,** tel: 1-0177 (national number).
**Johannesburg General Hospital,** tel: (011) 488-4911, fax: 643-1210.
**Gauteng Tourism Authority,** Airport: tel: (011) 390-3602/14; Newtown: tel: (011) 639-1600. Rosebank: tel: (011) 327-2000.
**Computicket,** tel: (011) 340-8000.
**First National Bank,** tel: 0860 112 244.
**AA of South Africa,** tel: 083 843 22.
**South African Tourism,** tel: (011) 895-3000.
**Johannesburg Tourism,** tel: (011) 214-0700.

## TRAVEL TIPS

A network of well-signposted roads and highways links the centres in this region. Speed limits apply to usual urban zones like schools and hospitals. As in crowded city areas worldwide, crime presents a growing problem. Common sense, however, goes a long way towards preventing potentially unpleasant situations. Below are some safety guidelines:
• Plan your itinerary before setting out.
• Don't leave your vehicle if it is bumped from behind, but rather proceed to a populated and well-lit area.
• Never park in poorly lit areas.
• Don't walk around alone after dusk.
• Leave your personal belongings and valuables safely stored in the hotel when you venture out.

**Below:** *Designed in grandiose style, the Gold Reef City casino complex in Johannesburg contains a casino, retail outlets and a four-star hotel.*

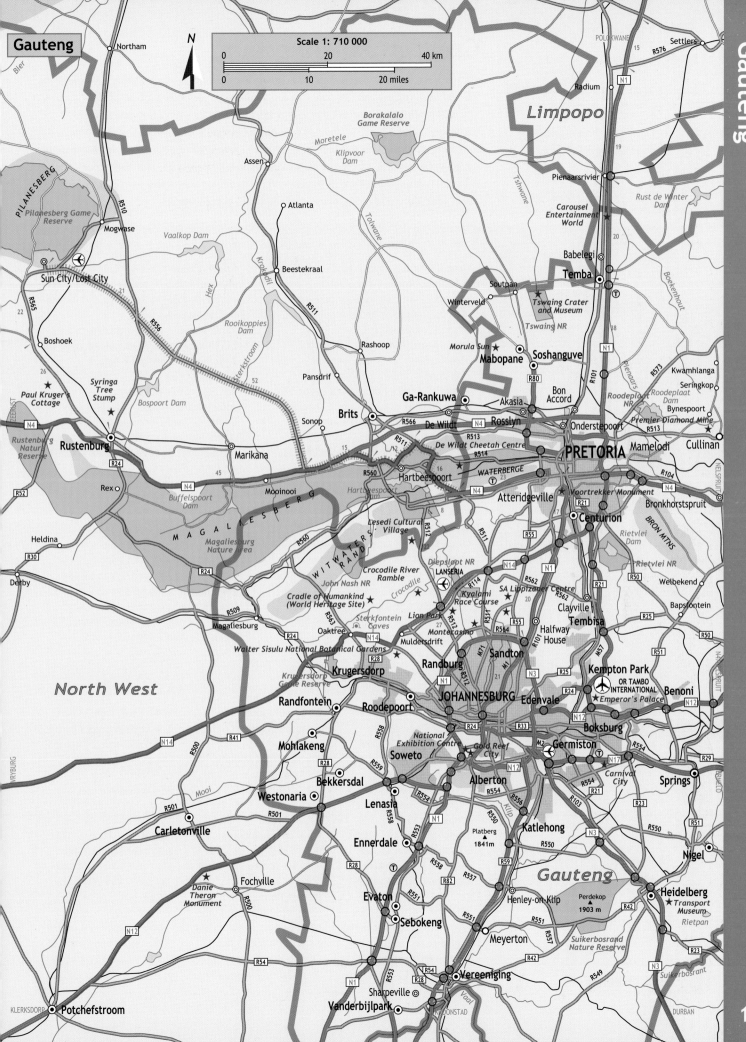

Scale 1: 710 000

0    20    40 km

0    10    20 miles

N

Limpopo

Bier

Northam

Pilanesberg Game Reserve

Mogwase

Sun City / Lost City

R565

R510

Boshoek

22

26

Paul Kruger's Cottage

Syringa Tree Stump

ZEERUST

N4

Rustenburg Nature Reserve

Rustenburg

R24

R52

Heldina

R30

Derby

R24

Rex

Buffelspoort Dam

MAGALIESBERG

Magaliesburg Nature Area

Vaalkop Dam

Krokodil

Hex

Assen

Atlanta

Beestekraal

Klipvoor Dam

Moretele

Borakalalo Game Reserve

Rooikoppies Dam

Sterkstroom

52

Bospoort Dam

Pansdrif

Rashoop

Sonop

Marikana

Mooinooi

R556

R511

Tolwane

Tshwane

Brits

Hartbeespoort Dam

R560

45

15

N4

16

Hartbeespoort

De Wildt

De Wildt Cheetah Centre

R566

Soutpan

Winterveld

Ga-Rankuwa

Akasia

Rosslyn

R513

R514

WATERBERGE

R80

Mabopane

Morula Sun

Soshanguve

Bon Accord

Onderstepoort

Polokwane

Settlers

R576

15

Radium

N1

19

Pienaarsrivier

Carousel Entertainment World

20

Babelegi

Temba

T

Tswaing Crater and Museum

Tswaing NR

Kwamhlanga

R573

Seringkop

Roodeplaat NR

Roodeplaat Dam

Byenspoort

Premier Diamond Mine

R101

88

N1

PRETORIA

Mamelodi

Cullinan

R513

R104

NELSPRUIT

North West

Magaliesberg

R509

R24

R563

Oaktree

N14

Sterkfontein Caves

Cradle of Humankind (World Heritage Site)

John Nash NR

WITWATERSRAND

Crocodile River Ramble

Crocodile

Diepsloot NR

LANSERIA

R512

R511

SA Lippizaner Centre

R562

Kyalami Race Course

R114

Walter Sisulu National Botanical Gardens

Muldersdrift

R28

Lion Park

Montecasino

27

R512

R564

Clayville

Tembisa

Halfway House

R55

N14

N1

R562

20

Atteridgeville

Voortrekker Monument

R21

Centurion

R55

Rietvlei Dam

BRON MTNS

Rietvlei NR

R50

Welbekend

Bapsfontein

R21

R25

Randfontein

Krugersdorp Game Reserve

Krugersdorp

Randburg

Sandton

M71

M1

JOHANNESBURG

Roodepoort

N1

R512

Mohlakeng

R41

R500

N14

R28

R558

National Exhibition Centre

Gold Reef City

Soweto

Bekkersdal

Westonaria

Lenasia

R558

R559

R553

N1

Edenvale

R24

R33

M2

Germiston

T

N17

Boksburg

R554

R24

M57

Kempton Park

OR TAMBO INTERNATIONAL

Emperor's Palace

Benoni

N12

R51

R50

Springs

R23

R51

Carletonville

R501

R501

Mooi

Danie Theron Monument

Fochville

R500

Evaton

Sebokeng

R551

R28

T

Ennerdale

R553

Alberton

R554

Katlehong

R556

Klip

R103

R21

R554

Carnival City

R29

VRYBURG

N12

KLERKSDORP

Potchefstroom

R54

R553

N1

R28

R54

Vanderbijlpark

Sharpeville

Vereeniging

Meyerton

R557

R551

Platberg 1841m

R59

Henley-on-Klip

R82

R557

R558

Perdekop 1903m

Suikerbosrand Nature Reserve

R42

Heidelberg

Transport Museum

Rietpan

Suikerbosrant

Gauteng

R550

R549

N3

R23

DURBAN

KROONSTAD

Vaal

NATAL SPRUIT

# Greater Johannesburg

*The huge yellow mine dumps and rusting headgear of the abandoned gold mines to the south of modern Johannesburg are evocative reminders of the days when the city was essentially a diggers' camp — a visit to Gold Reef City lets you relive the exciting gold-rush past. To the north, wealthy garden suburbs like Sandton and Randburg offer up-market shopping centres, fashionable boutiques, souvenir shops, an impressive range of cosmopolitan and ethnic restaurants, and numerous entertainment venues. Informal art and craft markets are regularly held in the many parks. For the golfer, there are a dozen challenging courses.*

## MAIN ATTRACTIONS

**Gold Reef City:** experience Johannesburg during the gold-rush days. Descend deep into a mine, visit the museums and the fairground, tel: (011) 248-6800.
**Brightwater Commons:** attractive complex with live entertainment, restaurants, shops and pubs.
**Market Theatre complex:** theatre and jazz venue in the city centre, and the location of Newtown Art Gallery, tel: (011) 832-1641.
**MuseuMAfrica:** displays and artefacts illustrate South Africa's turbulent history from prehistory to the present, tel: (011) 833-5624.
**Flea markets:** the Johannesburg (at the Market Theatre every Saturday 09:00-16:00) and Bruma Lake (daily 10:00-18:00) flea markets offer almost anything. Great for people watching.
**Soweto:** fascinating tours in South Africa's most famous township. For information call the Gauteng Tourism Authority, *see page 10.*

## EVENTS AND FESTIVALS

**South African PGA Golf Tournament:** International and Southern African golfing greats meet in **Jan** to fight it out for this prestigious title.
**Rand Show:** in **Apr** the National Exhibition Centre (southwest of Johannesburg) hosts the biggest consumer show in Africa, featuring local and international products.
**Johannesburg Pops Festival:** in **Apr** traditional and contemporary musicians, choirs and soloists get together for the most vibrant three-day outdoor concert in Southern Africa.
**International Eisteddfod of South Africa:** during **Sep/Oct** in the city of **Roodepoort** musicians and dancers from around the world compete for honours in this cultural event.
**Gay and Lesbian Pride:** original, largest local gay and lesbian celebration, **Sep.**
**Encounters:** South Africa's only film festival devoted exclusively to documentaries; **Jul-Aug,** features screenings, panel discussions and workshops.

## ACCOMMODATION

**Sandton Sun and Tower**, Sandton City, tel: (011) 780-5000, fax: 780-5002; luxurious accommodation.
**The Grace**, Rosebank, tel: (011) 280-7200, fax: 280-7474; small five-star hotel.
**Emperor's Palace**, Kempton Park, tel: (011) 928-1000; luxurious, up-market casino complex.
**Gold Reef Protea Hotel**, tel: (011) 248-5700, fax: (011) 248-5791; Victorian charm, located right in the theme park.
**City Lodge Morningside**, tel: (011) 884-9500, fax:

884-9440; just 30 min from the airport in lovely Sandton.
**Garden Court Milpark**, Auckland Park, tel: (011) 726-5100, fax: 726-5123; 6km (4 miles) from the city centre.
**Karos Johannesburger**, tel: (011) 725-3753, fax: 725-6309; located in the heart of town.
**Airport Formule 1**, tel: (011) 392-1453, fax: 974-3845; budget; close to the International Airport.
**City Lodge Airport**, tel: (011) 392-1750, fax: 392-

2644; 5 min from airport.
**The Cottages**, guesthouse and conference centre in Observatory, tel: (011) 487-2829.
**Ah Ha Guesthouse**, located in Bedfordview, 15 minutes for the airport, tel: (011) 616-3702.
**Lolo's Guesthouse**, tel: (011) 985-9183, cell: 082 332 2460; award-winning establishment where Mrs Mabitsela, a retired teacher, shares her wealth of first-hand knowledge of the turbulence in Soweto in the 70s with her guests.

---

**North West**

Rustenburg•

PRETORIA

JOHANNESBURG

*Gauteng*

Heidelberg•

---

| 346 km | PRETORIA | 0 km |
|---|---|---|
| | N1 | |
| | N1    N3 | |
| | 58 | |
| **JOHANNESBURG** | | |
| 288 | 16 | 58 |
| 272 | N12    N12 | 74 |
| Potchefstroom (101) | N3 | |
| 40 | Heidelberg (39) | |
| | Vereeniging | |
| 232 | | 114 |
| Vanderbijlpark   Sasolburg | | |
| | Heilbron (55) | |
| 28 | | |
| | R59 | |
| N1 | | |
| 204 | | 142 |
| Parys | | |
| | 101 | |
| Vredefort   N1 | | |
| R721 | | |
| 103 | | 243 |
| | 103 | |
| Kroonstad | | |
| 0 km | **WINBURG** | 346 km |

Greater Johannesburg

Scale 1: 200 000

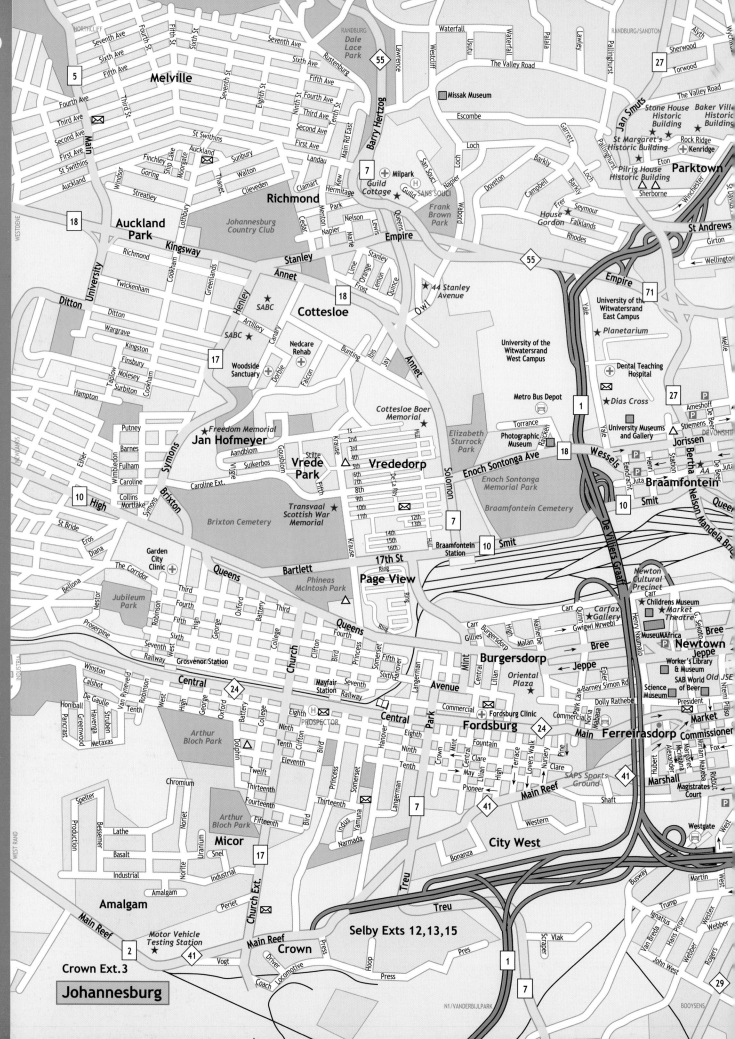

# Pretoria

*Handsome Pretoria is noted for its stately, historic homes, the impressive Union Buildings (home to major departments of the national government), its parks and gardens with their splendid wealth of flora, and for its tall jacaranda trees that transform the streets into a blaze of lilac each October/November, earning Pretoria its nickname, 'Jacaranda City'. The city is the administrative capital of the country, as well as a centre of research and learning. Within its limits lie the University of Pretoria; gigantic UNISA, among the world's largest distance-learning institutions; and Onderstepoort, an internationally renowned veterinary research institute.*

**Above:** *Summertime in Pretoria is heralded by a glory of lilac blossoms as the many jacaranda trees begin to flower, covering city streets and walks with a fragrant, pastel-coloured carpet.*

## MAIN ATTRACTIONS

**Union Buildings:** magnificent edifice designed by Sir Herbert Baker overlooking the city from Meintjieskop. To view the lovely gardens, tel: (012) 300-5200.

**Church Square:** historic town square framed by beautiful old buildings such as the Ou Raadsaal (parliament), Palace of Justice and SA Reserve Bank.

**Voortrekker Monument:** construction on Monument Hill, 6km (4 miles) from the city, commemorating the Great Trek of the 1830 pioneers.

**National Zoological Gardens:** Africa's largest zoological garden and houses an array of southern African and exotic animals. The zoo is open 365 days a year, tel: (012) 328-3265, www.zoo.ac.za

**Transvaal Museum of Natural History:** extensive displays, including the impressive 'Life's Genesis' and the Austin Roberts Bird Hall, tel: (012) 322-7632, fax: 322-7939.

**State Theatre:** on completion in 1981, this cultural complex, comprising five theatres and a public square, was the largest of its kind in the southern hemisphere, tel: (012) 392-4000, fax: 322-3913.

## ACCOMMODATION

**Centurion Lake Hotel**, 1001 Lenchen Avenue North, Centurion, tel: (012) 643-3600, fax: 643-3636.

**Southern Sun Pretoria**, cnr Beatrix and Church streets, Arcadia, tel: (012) 341-1571, fax: 440-7534; centrally located.

**Arcadia Hotel**, tel: (012) 326-9311, fax: 326-1067; beautifully situated right at the foot of the impressive Union Buildings.

**Garden Court Hatfield**, tel: (012) 342-1444, fax: 342-3492.

**Bentley's Country Lodge**, cnr Main Street and Brits Road, Akasia, tel: (012) 542-1751, fax: 542-3487.

**The Farm Inn**, Lynnwood Road, The Willows, tel: (012) 809-0266, fax: 809-0146; beautiful game farm close to the city and the Menlyn Park shopping and entertainment centre, next to Silverlakes Golf Club.

## USEFUL CONTACTS

**Pretoria Tourist Information Centre**, Church Square, tel: (012) 337-4487.

**International Embassies/Consulates**, all on dialling code (012):
• Australia, tel: 423-6000, fax: 342-4222
• France, tel: 425-1600, fax: 425-1609
• Germany, tel: 427-8900, fax: 343-9401
• Italy, tel: 423-0000, fax: 430-5547
• Netherlands, tel: 425-4500,
• Spain, tel: 344-3877, fax: 343-4891
• UK, tel: 421-7500, fax: 421 7555
• USA, tel: 431-4000, fax: 342-2299.

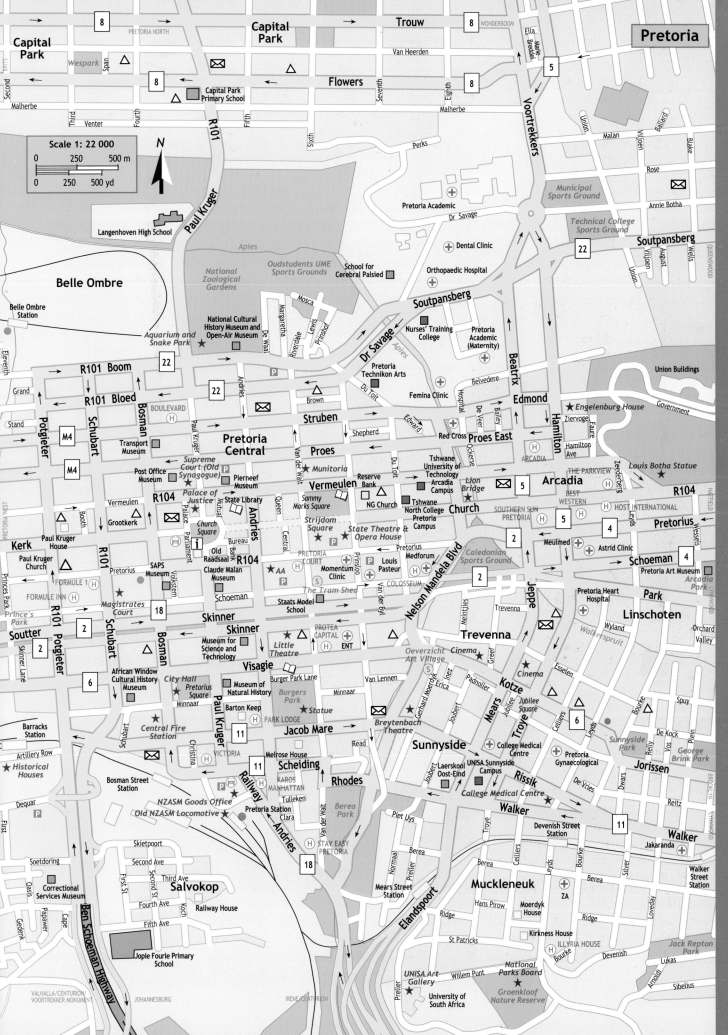

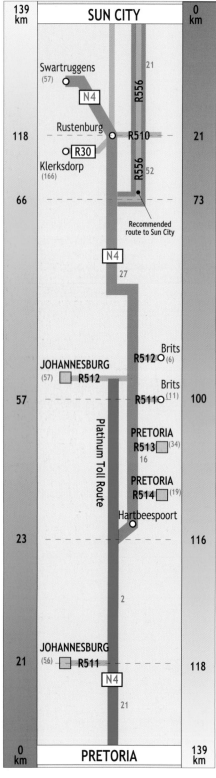

# Pilanesberg and Sun City

*The dramatic Lost City and Sun City leisure resort, one of South Africa's most glittering tourist venues featuring casinos, bars, restaurants, hotels, theatres, nightclubs and shops, is set among the lush vegetation of beautifully landscaped grounds, in what before was little more than desert territory. Apart from the 31,500m² (339,063ft²) Valley of the Waves, a man-made water park with soft sand beaches, waterslides, cascades and 1.8m-high (5.9ft) waves, the complex also offers an Arizona Desert-style golf course where crocodiles lie in wait at the 13th hole, and another at the Gary Player Country Club, venue of the annual Nedbank Golf Challenge. Musicians such as Queen and Elton John have also performed at the Sun City Super Bowl, a large auditorium which seats 6000. Pilanesberg National Park north of Sun City has some 10,000 head of wildlife including the Big Five — buffalo, rhino (black and white), elephant, lion and leopard — and over 300 bird species. This game-rich habitat lies within four concentric mountain rings, the relics of an ancient volcano. In the centre of the bowl is Mankwe Dam, a favourite hippo haunt. The park is traversed by a network of game-viewing roads; guided walks and drives are conducted and hot-air balloon trips can be organized. This wonderful park is the result of 'Operation Genesis', a successful game-stocking venture. A visit to the aviary at Manyane Gate should not be missed.*

## ACCOMMODATION

**Sun City complex**, tel: (014) 557-1000.
**The Cascades Hotel**, tel: (014) 557-5840.
**Palace of the Lost City Hotel**, tel: (014) 557-4307. Luxurious extravagance.
**The Cabanas Hotel**, tel: (014) 557-1580. Family orientated and affordable.
**Sun City Hotel**, tel: (014) 557-5110. Five-star comfort surrounded by sub-tropical gardens.

**Pilanesberg National Park**, tel: (014) 555-1600.
**Bakubung Game Lodge**, tel: (014) 552-6000, fax: 552-6300; thatched rooms around a hippo pool in a private game reserve.
**Kwa Maritane Lodge**, tel: (014) 552-5100, fax: 552-5333; luxurious accommodation in the African bush.

## USEFUL CONTACTS

**Pilanesberg National Park**, tel: (014) 555-1600; for the real bush experience.

**Below:** *Fabled to be the royal residence of an ancient king, the Palace of the Lost City rises dramatically out of the surrounding African bush, like the legendary temple of a mysterious civilization.*

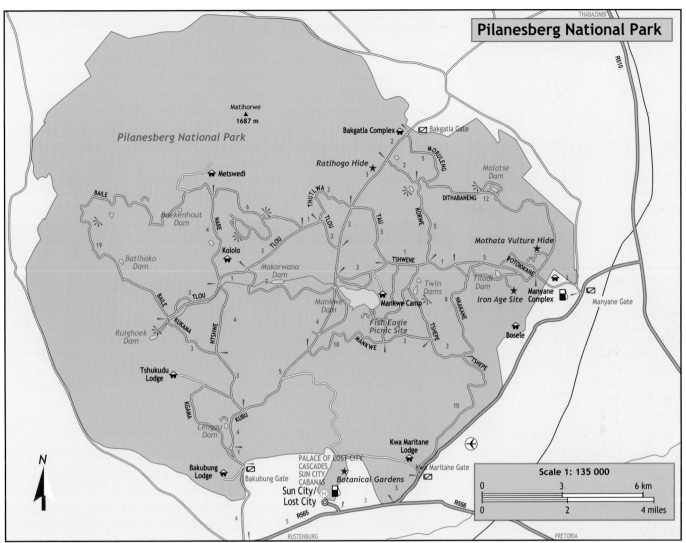

Pilanesberg National Park

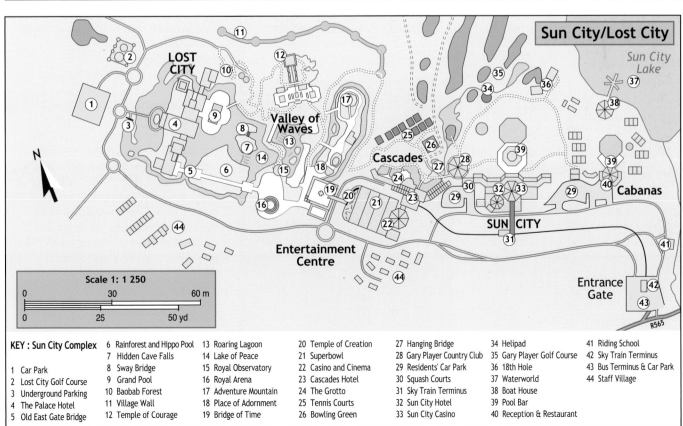

Sun City/Lost City

Scale 1: 1 250

| KEY : Sun City Complex | | | | | |
|---|---|---|---|---|---|
| 1 Car Park | 6 Rainforest and Hippo Pool | 13 Roaring Lagoon | 20 Temple of Creation | 27 Hanging Bridge | 34 Helipad | 41 Riding School |
| 2 Lost City Golf Course | 7 Hidden Cave Falls | 14 Lake of Peace | 21 Superbowl | 28 Gary Player Country Club | 35 Gary Player Golf Course | 42 Sky Train Terminus |
| 3 Underground Parking | 8 Sway Bridge | 15 Royal Observatory | 22 Casino and Cinema | 29 Residents' Car Park | 36 18th Hole | 43 Bus Terminus & Car Park |
| 4 The Palace Hotel | 9 Grand Pool | 16 Royal Arena | 23 Cascades Hotel | 30 Squash Courts | 37 Waterworld | 44 Staff Village |
| 5 Old East Gate Bridge | 10 Baobab Forest | 17 Adventure Mountain | 24 The Grotto | 31 Sky Train Terminus | 38 Boat House | |
| | 11 Village Wall | 18 Place of Adornment | 25 Tennis Courts | 32 Sun City Hotel | 39 Pool Bar | |
| | 12 Temple of Courage | 19 Bridge of Time | 26 Bowling Green | 33 Sun City Casino | 40 Reception & Restaurant | |

# Kruger National Park

*South Africa's premier wildlife sanctuary covers more than 20,000 km² (7720 sq miles) — an area about the size of Wales and larger than the state of Israel. Because this vast, wild expanse encompasses many different habitats, it is a haven for more varieties of wildlife than any other conservation area in Africa. Among the estimated 140 mammal species occurring here are the Big Five: lion (approximately 1500), elephant (about 13,500), leopard (around 1000), buffalo (27,000), and rhino, both black and white. Other large wildlife populations include zebra, wildebeest, giraffe, hippo and crocodile, as well as some 500 bird species. If you are lucky, you may even spot a pack of the increasingly rare wild dogs.*

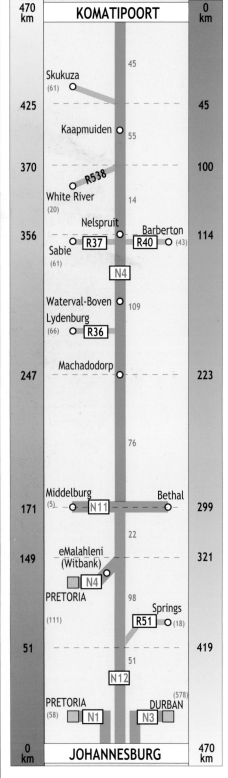

## TRAVEL TIPS

An extensive network, consisting of about 880km (550 miles) of tarred surface and 1700km (1060 miles) of gravel road, traverses the park, providing effective access to all areas of the Kruger. Should you experience any car trouble, vehicle breakdown services are available at Skukuza and Letaba camps. A few general safety guidelines have to be observed by all visitors:

• Malaria treatment should be started prior to entering this area (consult your physician), and use insect repellent.
• Stay on the designated roads or tracks.
• Keep to the speed limit.
• Do not leave your vehicle.
• Don't injure, feed or disturb wildlife.
• Littering is an offence.
• Be sure to arrive at your rest camp by the stipulated time before sunset.

## MAIN ATTRACTIONS

**The Big Five** can be viewed in their natural environment. To view, try the **Pafuri area** in the far north. **Water holes** attract a steady parade of wildlife. Overnight visitors have a choice of 20 or so comfortable, tree-shaded **rest camps**, of which **Skukuza** is the largest, boasting all the amenities of a small town. **Olifants Camp**, perched on high cliffs, offers splendid vistas. Smaller and more intimate are the **bush camps**. **Tshokwane** is among several attractive **picnic spots**; Nwanetsi, which overlooks the Sweni River, is an especially rewarding **look-out post**. A number of **wilderness trails** offer the ultimate bush experience. **Private game lodges** provide luxury, personal service and superb game-viewing. Popular spots include Sabi Sabi, Londolozi and Mala Mala. Check out the following website for a list of lodges in the area, www.places.co.za

**Left:** *Elephants should always be approached with caution. Warning signals, which include a raised trunk and flapping ears, should never be ignored. Elephants are voracious feeders which daily consume up to 272kg (600 lb) of grass, tender shoots and bark from trees. The elephant's sensitive trunk can even detect water underground. An adult elephant can drink up to 200 litres of water in a single session.*

## ACCOMMODATION

Over 20 pleasant, clean and safe rest camps are located within the park. For reservations contact **South African National Parks**, tel: (012) 428-9111, fax: 426-5500, website: www.sanparks.org

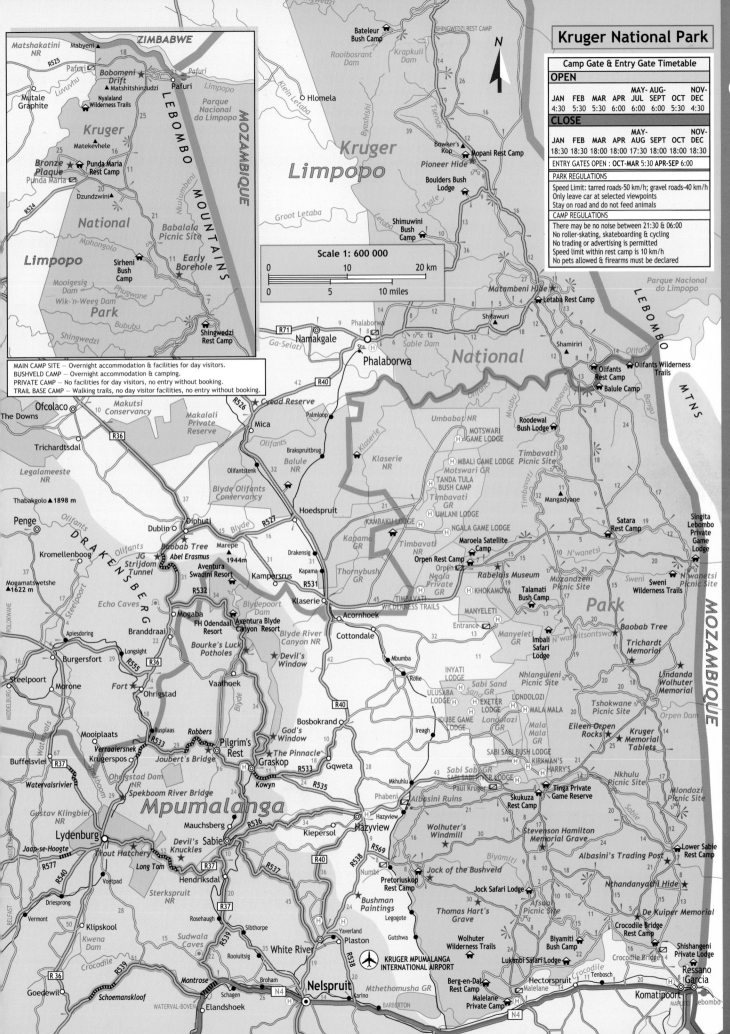

# Kruger National Park

Scale 1: 600 000

| 0 | 10 | 20 km |

| 0 | 5 | 10 miles |

## Camp Gate & Entry Gate Timetable

### OPEN

| | JAN | FEB | MAR | APR | MAY-JUL | AUG-SEPT | OCT | NOV-DEC |
|---|---|---|---|---|---|---|---|---|
| | 4:30 | 5:30 | 5:30 | 6:00 | 6:00 | 6:00 | 5:30 | 4:30 |

### CLOSE

| | JAN | FEB | MAR | APR | MAY-AUG | SEPT | OCT | NOV-DEC |
|---|---|---|---|---|---|---|---|---|
| | 18:30 | 18:30 | 18:00 | 18:00 | 17:30 | 18:00 | 18:00 | 18:30 |

ENTRY GATES OPEN : OCT-MAR 5:30  APR-SEP 6:00

### PARK REGULATIONS
Speed Limit: tarred roads-50 km/h; gravel roads-40 km/h
Only leave car at selected viewpoints
Stay on road and do not feed animals

### CAMP REGULATIONS
There may be no noise between 21:30 & 06:00
No roller-skating, skateboarding & cycling
No trading or advertising is permitted
Speed limit within rest camp is 10 km/h
No pets allowed & firearms must be declared

MAIN CAMP SITE — Overnight accommodation & facilities for day visitors.
BUSHVELD CAMP — Overnight accommodation & camping.
PRIVATE CAMP — No facilities for day visitors, no entry without booking.
TRAIL BASE CAMP — Walking trails, no day visitor facilities, no entry without booking.

# Mpumalanga Drakensberg

*Mountainous terrain, misty forests, bushveld and endless views are the compelling features of this escarpment region far to the east of Gauteng, across the great Highveld plateau. For sheer scenic beauty, few parts of the Southern African subcontinent can compare with the Great Escarpment, a spectacular wonderland of buttresses, sculpted peaks and deep ravines. The Olifants and Crocodile rivers and a score of their tributaries run through verdant valleys. One tributary, the Blyde River, over centuries carved a canyon that now ranks as one of Africa's great scenic splendours.*

## MAIN ATTRACTIONS

**Blyde River Canyon:** a majestic gorge whose sheer cliff faces plunge to the water far below.

**Bourke's Luck Potholes:** a fantasia of hollowed-out rocks.

**Pilgrim's Rest:** town born out of the 1870 gold rush, now a quaint living museum.

**Jock of the Bushveld:** trail begins in Graskop for the heroic dog in the novel by Sir Percy FitzPatrick.

**God's Window:** for the most magnificent views of the area.

**Mount Sheba:** beautiful forest reserve high in the mountains.

**Magoebaskloof:** large tracts of thick indigenous forest.

**Long Tom Pass:** spectacular pass between Sabie and Lydenburg.

**Echo Caves:** archaeological evidence of earlier inhabitants.

**The Trout Triangle:** area around Waterval-Boven, Dullstroom and Lydenburg; popular with nature-lovers and the fly-fishing elite.

**Khamai Reptile Park:** with snakes, lizards and crocodiles. Interesting presentations and commentaries and, for those so inclined, the chance of handling a snake.

## TRAVEL TIPS

The region has an excellent network of roads. Travelling from Johannesburg to Nelspruit and the escarpment, take the R22 and then the N4 near eMalahleni (Witbank); from Pretoria take the N4 direct. The R40 leads from Nelspruit north into the escarpment. Alternatively, follow the N1 national highway from Pretoria; turn right at Polokwane (Pietersburg) on the R71 for Tzaneen and the central region of the Kruger National Park (around Phalaborwa). If you intend travelling into the far northern region of the park, take the R524 at Louis Trichardt (Makhado). Please note: this is a **malaria** area so ensure that the necessary precautions are taken before travelling into this area; for more information on the hazards, consult your physician.

## ACCOMMODATION

**Mount Sheba Hotel**, west of Pilgrim's Rest, tel: (013) 768-1241, fax: 768-1248; luxury hotel.

**Sabi River Sun**, close to Paul Kruger Gate, tel: (013) 737-7311, fax: 737-7314; 18-hole golf course.

**Pine Lake Sun**, White River, tel: (013) 750-0709, fax: 751-3873; on the edge of a lake; golf course.

**Royal Hotel**, Pilgrim's Rest, tel: (013) 768-1100, fax: 768-1188; stay in a national monument.

**Critchley Hackle Lodge**, Dullstroom, tel: (013) 254-0149, fax: 254-0262.

**Malapo Country Lodge**, Lydenburg, tel: (013) 235-1056, fax: (013) 235-2398; with ASTRO Boma (open-air Observatory) where African star lore comes alive.

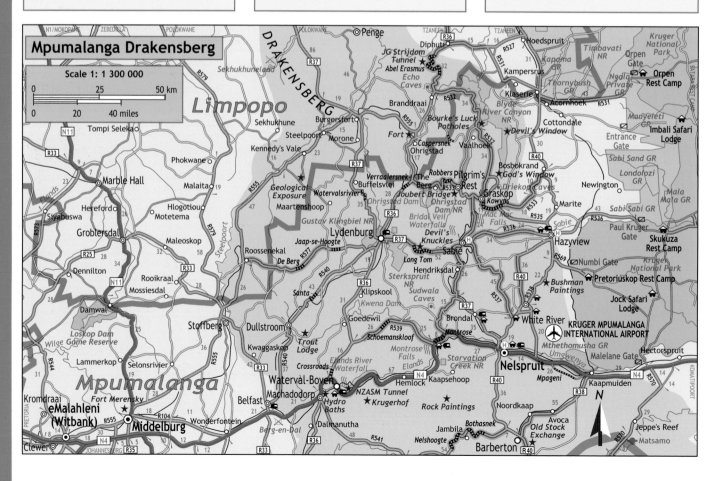

# Nelspruit

Largest town in, and capital of, Mpumalanga is Nelspruit, set on the Crocodile River in the warm, undulating grasslands below the escarpment and centre of a beautiful and immensely fertile area. It's an attractive little city of wide streets lined with poinciana trees that, during the summer months, are ablaze with deep red blossoms. Nelspruit is the last major town on the southern route to the Kruger National Park; among its attractions are excellent hotels and restaurants, modern shopping centres and speciality outlets that cater well for the tourist.

## MAIN ATTRACTIONS

**Lowveld Botanical Gardens:** on the Crocodile River, supporting over 600 species of indigenous flora.

**Lowveld Herbarium:** adjacent to the Gardens; of interest to the botanist as well as the layperson.

**Sudwala Caves:** dramatic cave formations and an interesting dinosaur park, about 40km (25 miles) northwest of Nelspruit.

**Riverside Trail:** self-guided 4km (2.5-mile) hike along the Crocodile River, with some lovely waterfalls.

**Farm stalls:** roadside stalls around the town sell fresh fruit and curios.

**Barberton Museum Complex:** opened in 1994; gives a comprehensive picture of the history, geology, archaeology and ethnology of the region.

## ACCOMMODATION

**Cybele Forest Lodge**, R40, White River, tel: (013) 764-1823, fax: 764-9510; exclusive retreat surrounded by nature.

**Protea Hotel The Winkler**, tel: (013) 751-5068, fax: 751-5044; in the beautiful White River area.

**Mercure Premier Lodge**, Graniet Street, Nelspruit, tel: (013) 741-4222.

**The Rest Country Lodge**, tel: (013) 744-9991, fax: (013) 744-9472; luxury suites near Nelspruit.

**Lowveld Lodge**, Tom Lawrence Street, White River, tel: (013) 750-0206.

## USEFUL CONTACTS

**Mpumalanga Tourism and Parks Agency**, tel: (013) 752-7001.

## WATERFALL ROUTE

There are some beautiful waterfalls in the Sabie-Graskop area about 50km (31 miles) north of Nelspruit. The falls are worth a visit and are easily accessible on a good road network. Among the best falls to view are:

**Bridal Veil:** a delicate spray of water surrounded by a forest echoing with the calls of many birds; 7km (4.2 miles) north of Sabie.

**Mac Mac:** twin cascades plunge 56m (185ft) into a deep, green ravine.

**Lone Creek:** hidden some 68m (222ft) in a beautiful, misty forest.

**Horseshoe:** a national monument.

**Berlin:** plunges about 48m (158ft) into a deep pool.

**Lisbon:** picturesque double waterfall in a setting of special beauty.

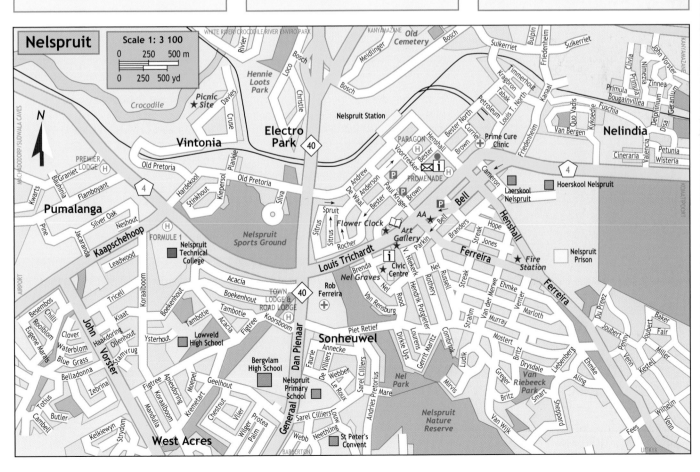

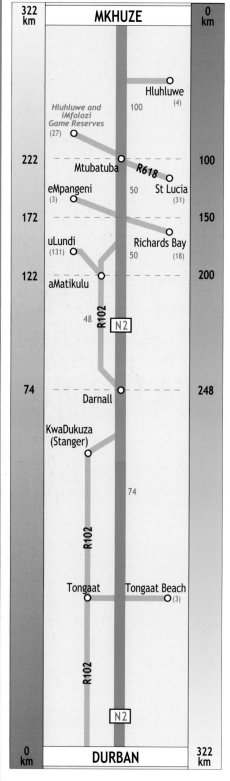

# KwaZulu-Natal North Coast

*R*emarkable for its rich fauna and flora, northern KwaZulu-Natal boasts some of South Africa's finest game reserves (among them the Hluhluwe and iMfolozi Game Reserves, oldest of South Africa's many wildlife sanctuaries) and one of the world's great wetland and marine conservation areas, now a World Heritage Site, the iSimangaliso Wetland Park (St Lucia). Just north of Durban, along the Dolphin Coast that stretches for 90km (55 miles) up to the uThukela River mouth, lies the up-market resort town of uMhlanga Rocks. Beyond lies the area historically known as Zululand, whose largest centre and industrial hub is Richards Bay, notable for its busy deep-water harbour. The beaches, fringed by tropical vegetation, attract sun-bathers, anglers, divers and boating enthusiasts.

## MAIN ATTRACTIONS

**Beaches:** some excellent beaches north and south of Durban include uMhlanga Rocks, Tongaat, Ballito, Shaka's Rock, Salt Rock, Shelly Beach, North Beach (Margate) and uVongo.

**Natal Sharks Board:** in uMhlanga; enjoy an informative audiovisual presentation. Book in advance.

**Lake Sibaya:** South Africa's largest natural freshwater lake.

**The Elephant Coast:** declared a World Heritage Site and among the world's most ecologically diverse sanctuaries. Contact St Lucia Tourism Association, tel: (035) 590-1247.

**Maputaland Reserves:** host some of the greatest concentrations of wildlife in South Africa.

The **Hluhluwe and iMfolozi Game Reserves:** famed for their rhino conservation programme and offering a haven for the Big Five, tel: (035) 562-0848 (Hilltop Camp), tel: (035) 550-8476 (Mpila Camp).

**Phinda Resource Reserve:** one of the best ecotourism destinations in South Africa, tel: (035) 562-0271, fax: 562-0399.

**Sodwana Bay:** marine wonderland, the best diving venue in South Africa, tel: (035) 571-0051/2/3.

**Shakaland:** model of a traditional Zulu village in the Nkwaleni Valley; includes culinary specialities, tribal dancing and traditional healers. Protea Hotel Shakaland: tel: (035) 460-0912.

## TRAVEL TIPS

The N2 runs parallel to, but mostly out of sight of, the coast to the eMpangeni-Richards Bay area (north of Durban), and then sweeps inland to the Swaziland border. Major roads in Zululand are tarred; most of the minor ones (including those in the game reserves) are gravel and generally in a satisfactory condition.

## USEFUL CONTACTS

**Dolphin Coast Publicity Association,** tel: (032) 946-1997.
**Isle of Capri Cruises,** tel: (031) 337-7751, fax: (031) 305-3099; deep-sea cruises and fishing trips.
**Natal Sharks Board,** tel: (031) 566-0400.

**Below:** *The golden sands of St Lucia.*

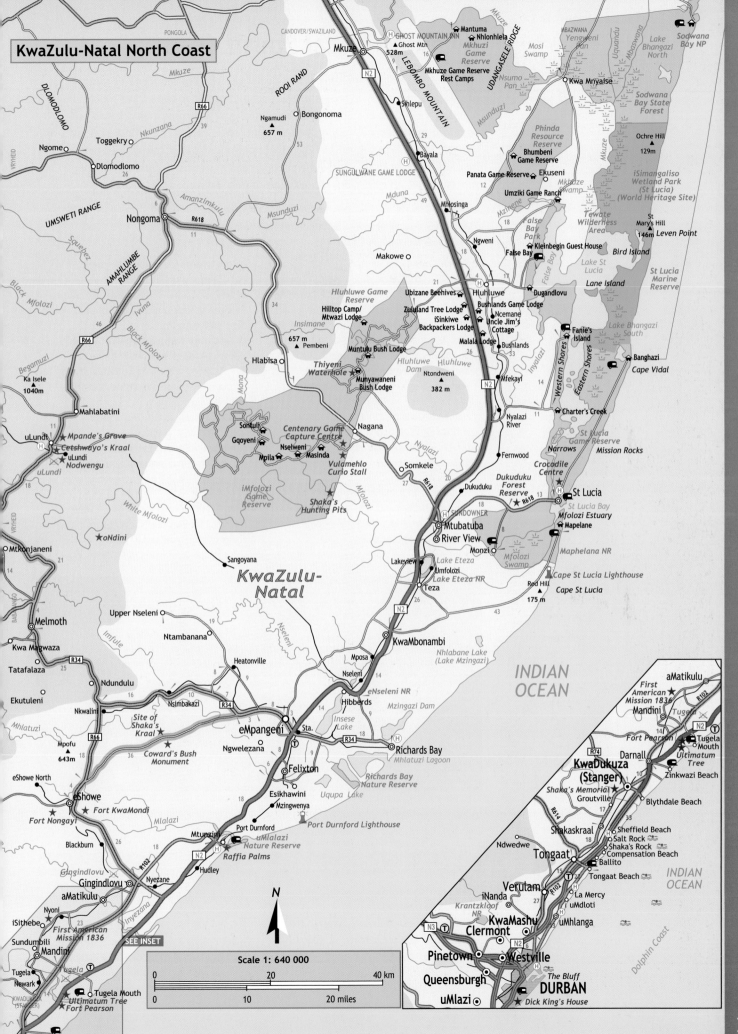

# KwaZulu-Natal North Coast

KwaZulu-Natal

INDIAN OCEAN

Scale 1: 640 000

SEE INSET

# KwaZulu-Natal South Coast

*T*he seaboard running south from Durban to the Eastern Cape border, or Mtamvuna River, is known as the South Coast. It is one of the southern hemisphere's most entrancing holiday regions, a subtropical wonderland of wide, unspoilt beaches lapped by the warm blue waters of the Indian Ocean, of a lushly green hinterland, and of a score and more sunlit towns, villages and hamlets, each with its special personality and attractions. Part of the long shoreline, which runs from Hibberdene to Port Edward, is also referred to as the Hibiscus Coast.

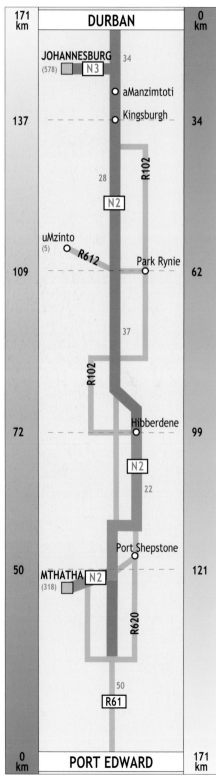

## MAIN ATTRACTIONS

### South Coast
**Kingsburgh:** five seaside resorts popular for their white sands and shark-protected bathing.
**uMkomaas:** a championship golf course and floodlit tidal pool.
**Scottburgh:** a charming beach, and fascinating Crocworld nearby.
**Vernon Crookes Nature Reserve:** lush sanctuary for various antelope.

### Hibiscus Coast
**Hibberdene:** lagoon, woodland-fringed beaches, amusement park.
**uMzumbe:** excellent family hotel; rock and surf angling.
**Banana Beach:** safe bathing and very good surfing.
**Bendigo:** four seaside resorts geared towards holiday-makers.

**uMtentweni:** for a quiet getaway.
**Port Shepstone:** at the mouth of the Mzimkulu River; offers excellent bowling greens and one of South Africa's best golf courses.
**Oribi Gorge Nature Reserve:** some 20km (14 miles) inland from Port Shepstone — a striking canyon carved through layers of sandstone by the Mzimkulwana River.
**uVongo:** lively little resort in an idyllic tropical setting.
**Margate:** very popular seaside town, but it can get crowded.
**Ramsgate:** magnificent lagoon and a long beach.
**Port Edward:** charming town in the former Transkei, with a pleasant beach; close to the Wild Coast Sun.

**Above:** *Scottburgh is a popular holiday resort on the South Coast. The lovely beach offers safe bathing, as well as some fine angling spots.*

## USEFUL CONTACTS

**Hospital GJ Crookes**, Scottburgh, tel: (039) 978-7000.
**Hibiscus Coast Tourism**, Margate, tel: (039) 312-2322, fax: 312-1886.
**Scottburgh Tourism**, tel: (039) 976-1364, fax: 978-3114.

## TRAVEL TIPS

Towns and resorts are linked to Durban by the N2 as far as Port Shepstone, while the R61 leads to Port Edward. Both roads are in good condition, though inland roads can be a little rough and caution is advised.

## KwaZulu-Natal South Coast

Scale 1: 640 000

| 0 | 20 | 40 km |

| 0 | 10 | 20 miles |

INDIAN OCEAN

N

Eastern Cape

KwaZulu-Natal

# Durban and Pietermaritzburg

*The city of Durban is South Africa's third largest metropolis, foremost seaport (the harbour is ranked ninth in the world in terms of size and traffic) and among the country's most popular holiday destinations. Durban and its subtropical surrounds offer many varied attractions: the beachfront, known as the Golden Mile, with its superb beaches (protected by anti-shark nets) for sunbathing, swimming and surfing; hotels, nightspots, restaurants, glittering shopping malls, pleasant parks and, in parts, an appealingly exotic atmosphere conferred by the city's large Indian community.*

## ACCOMMODATION

**Royal Hotel**, 267 Smith Street, tel: (031) 333-6000, fax: 333-6002; one of the best hotels in Durban; very luxurious.
**Hilton Hotel**, city centre, tel: (031) 336-8100. One of Durban's most luxurious hotels.
**Garden Court South Beach**, tel: (031) 337-2231, fax: 337-4640; stylish and comfortable.
**Garden Court Marine Parade**, tel: (031) 337-3341, fax: 332-9885.
**Balmoral Hotel**, Durban Beachfront, tel: (031) 368-5940, fax: 368-5955; situated right across the road from the beach.
**Protea Hotel Imperial**, 224 Loop Street, Pietermaritzburg, tel: (033) 342-6551, fax: 342-9796; central; colonial atmosphere.
**Crossways Country Inn**, Old Howick Road, just north of Pietermaritzburg, tel: (033) 343-3267, fax: 343-3273; English pub atmosphere.
**Rawdon's**, Old Main Road, Nottingham Road, tel: (033) 266-6044, fax: 266-6048; exquisite English country-style homestead.

## MAIN ATTRACTIONS

**Golden Mile:** fabulous holiday playground stretching along the sandy Indian Ocean shoreline.
**uShaka Marine World:** on the Golden Mile, popular aquarium-dolphinarium, tel: (031) 328-8000.
**Fitzsimon's Snake Park:** home to many snake species, as well as crocodiles.
**Victoria Street Indian Market:** colourful and exotic place of bargain and barter.
**uMgeni River Bird Park:** rated third best of the world's bird parks, tel: (031) 579-4600.
**Gandhi Settlement:** visit the renovated farm where Gandhi once resided; situated in iNanda.
**Gateway shopping centre:** 10 minutes north of Durban. Here you can surf, rockclimb, enjoy a meal and shop.
**Port Natal Maritime Museum:** on the Victoria Embankment; interesting exhibits dealing with the city's seafaring tradition, tel: (031) 311-2230.
**Pietermaritzburg:** quaint colonial-style town; fine architecture; interesting museums. Home to two internationally renowned sports events, the Dusi Canoe Marathon and the Comrades Marathon.

## EVENTS AND FESTIVALS

**Howick: Midmar Mile** swim marathon, held in **January**, sometimes **February**.
**Comrades Marathon:** famous marathon in **June** (Durban to Pietermaritzburg the one year, vice versa the following one).
**Durban July Handicap:** prestigious horse-racing event in **July**.
**Mr Price Pro:** world-renowned annual surfing contest held at New Pier in **June/July**.

## USEFUL CONTACTS

**Addington Hospital**, tel: (031) 327-2000, fax: 368-3300.
**Durban Tourism**, Tourist Junction, 160 Pine Street, Durban, tel: (031) 304-4934.
**uShaka Marine World**, the Point, Durban, tel: (031) 328-8000, www.ushakamarineworld.co.za
**Pietermaritzburg Tourism**, tel: (033) 345-1348, fax: 394-3535.

**Right:** *The Paddling Pools form part of Durban's sparkling Golden Mile. Other attractions on offer here include colourful markets, numerous restaurants, scenic walkways and fountains.*

## TRAVEL TIPS

Durban's international airport is 15 minutes from the city centre. It is linked to all other major South African centres by a network of national roads. The N2 leads south and then west along the coast, through Port Elizabeth to Cape Town. The N3 takes the traveller northwest through Pietermaritzburg and Harrismith to Johannesburg.

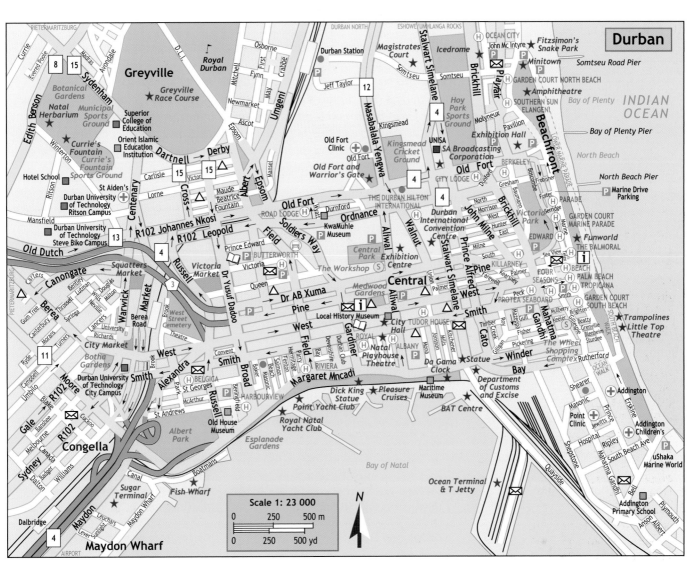

**Durban**

Scale 1: 23 000

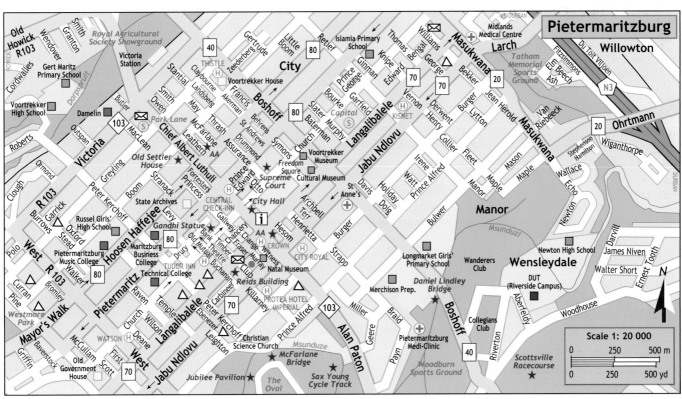

**Pietermaritzburg**

Scale 1: 20 000

# KwaZulu-Natal Drakensberg

*S*outh Africa's highest mountain range, the Drakensberg is a massive and strikingly beautiful rampart of deep gorges, pinnacles and saw-edged ridges, caves, overhangs and balancing rocks. In the winter months its upper levels lie deep in snow, but clustered among the foothills far below, in undulating grassland, is a score of resort hotels established and run for the most part for family holiday-makers. People come for the fresh, clean mountain air; for the walks, climbs and drives; for the gentler sports (trout fishing, golf, bowls and horseback riding); and for casual relaxation in the most exquisite surrounds.

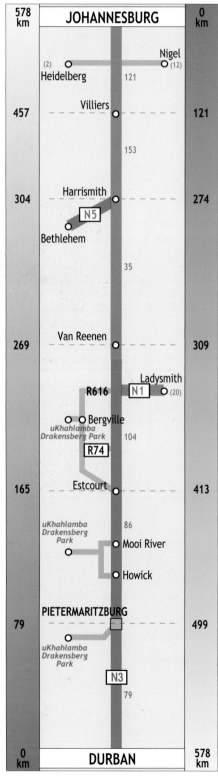

## ACCOMMODATION

**Cathedral Peak Hotel**, Winterton, tel: (036) 488-1888, fax: 488-1889; set amid spectacular peaks.
**Drakensberg Sun Hotel**, Winterton, tel: (036) 468-1000, fax: 468-1224; wonderful views.
**Little Switzerland Hotel**, between Bergville and Harrismith, tel: (036) 438-6220, fax: 438-6222; view of the spectacular Amphitheatre.

**Sani Pass Hotel**, Himeville, tel: (033) 702-1320, fax: 702-0220; 800ha (1977 acres) situated at the foot of Sani Pass.
**Champagne Castle Hotel**, tel: (036) 468-1063, fax: 468-1306; guided walks; golf course.
**Orion Mont-Aux-Sources Hotel**, tel: (036) 438-8000; 7km (4.3 miles) from the Royal Natal National Park.

## MAIN ATTRACTIONS

**Royal Natal National Park:** an extensive and beautiful floral and wildlife sanctuary. Excursions to the Mont-Aux-Sources plateau and the spectacular uThukela Falls, the country's highest waterfall.
**Champagne Castle:** a magnificent peak and one of the Drakensberg's easier climbs.
**Giant's Castle Game Reserve:** in the central Drakensberg, a scenic wonderland famous for its Bushman (San) rock art and raptor conservation programmes.
**Ndedema Gorge:** 'place of rolling thunder'; a magnificent gorge renowned for its rock art.
**Himeville Nature Reserve:** in the southern Drakensberg; a paradise for trout fishermen.
**The Midlands Meander:** a scenic route takes travellers through Meander outlets and picturesque villages. See art and craft studios, herb and flower farms, country pubs, breweries, and much more!

## USEFUL CONTACTS

**Drakensberg Tourism Association**, near Bergville, tel: (036) 448-1557.
**Central Drakensberg Information Centre**, tel: (036) 488-1207.
**Mountain Club of SA**, (KZN section) tel: (031) 260-1077.
**Drakensberg Boys Choir School**, tel: (036) 468-1012, except during school holidays.
**Midlands Meander Tourism**, for information tel: (033) 330-7260; website: www.midlandsmeander.co.za

**Right:** *The impressive Giant's Castle, formed by vast lava outpourings of the Drakensberg Basalt Formation (to a thickness of more than 1000m) is just one of the formations to be found in the beautiful Drakensberg mountain range.*

# Historic Battlefields

*F*or most of the 19th century, the KwaZulu-Natal battlefields region was a bloody battlefield, as Zulu, Boer and Briton fought for territorial supremacy. Military enthusiasts will find the Battlefields Route (which includes the sites of Blood River, iSandlwana, Rorke's Drift, uLundi, Majuba Hill, Talana, Elandslaagte, Tugela Heights, Colenso, Ladysmith and Spioenkop) fascinating. Some of the most dramatic confrontations occurred in the triangular area bounded by Estcourt in the south, Volksrust in the north, and Vryheid to the east.

## THE BATTLEFIELDS ROUTE

**Blood River (1838):** the final and decisive clash between the Zulus and the Voortrekker settlers during the Boer migration into Natal. Raw courage proved no match for superior firepower — more than 3000 Zulus perished on the field; Boer losses amounted to just three wounded.

**iSandlwana (1879):** part of a British invading force was annihilated by a 24,000-strong *impi* (army); only a handful of the 1000-plus redcoats survived.

**Rorke's Drift (1879):** a bitterly fought skirmish in which a small British garrison held out against wave after wave of Zulu *impi*. Between them, the defenders earned 11 Victoria Crosses.

**Majuba Hill (1881):** final battle of the brief Anglo-Transvaal war, in which a Boer force of part-time soldiers drove the British regulars from the slopes of the high hill, inflicting severe casualties. The British commander, Sir George Colley, is thought to have committed suicide during the retreat.

**Spioenkop (1900):** the Anglo-Boer War's bloodiest battle, savagely fought between Boer and Briton for control of the strategic hill on the route leading to the besieged Ladysmith. Casualties were high on both sides; the Boers eventually prevailed.

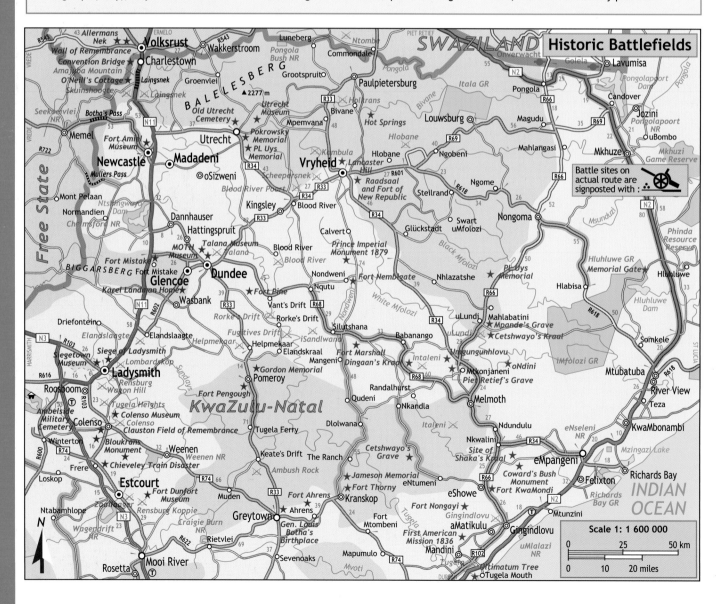

# Wild Coast

Southwestwards from the KwaZulu-Natal border lies the Transkei region, its rugged seaboard known as the Wild Coast — an unspoilt and quite beautiful 280km (174-mile) long wilderness of beaches and secluded bays, lagoons and estuaries (an impressive 18 rivers find their way to the Indian Ocean along the coastal strip), imposing cliffs and rocky reefs that probe, finger-like, out to sea. Rolling green hills and patches of dense vegetation grace the hinterland. Largest of its seaside villages are Port St Johns and Coffee Bay; most prominent resort, the superb Wild Coast Sun.

## TRAVEL TIPS

The N2 bisects this region, passing northeast to southwest from Port Shepstone through Kokstad, Mount Frere, Umtata and Butterworth, where grocery supplies and petrol can be obtained. The gravel roads leading down to the coast can be rather taxing on both vehicle and driver. Beware of straying animals.

## ACCOMMODATION

**Wild Coast Sun**, Transkei region, tel: (039) 305-9111, fax: 305-2778; glitz and glamour.
**Trennery's Hotel**, tel: (047) 498-0004; beautifully situated on Great Kei River, Kentani district.

**Above:** *The strange detached cliff known as Hole-in-the-Wall is a well-known spot not far from Coffee Bay on the beautiful Wild Coast.*

## MAIN ATTRACTIONS

**Wild Coast Sun:** an extravagant, luxury hotel-casino complex situated right on the beachfront.
**Hole-in-the-Wall:** a short drive south of Coffee Bay stands a massive detached cliff with a small arched opening through which the surf thunders.
**Mazeppa Bay:** palm trees line three wide beaches; the scuba diving, snorkelling and fishing spots are superb.
**Qhorha Mouth:** a good beach with interesting rock pools, close to the hotel. In the **Dwesa** and **Cwebe nature reserves** buffalo, eland and warthog roam the combined forest and grassland, while crocodiles patrol the rivers.
**Fishing:** catches range from kob, blacktail bronze bream and shad to barracuda and trophy-sized sharks.

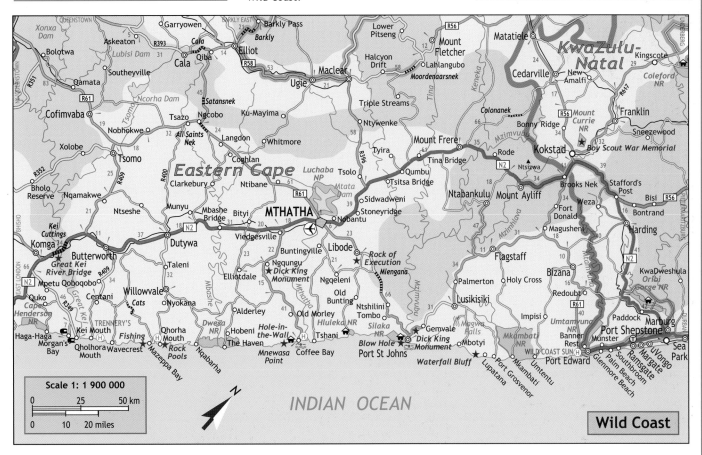

# Eastern Cape

*The region, extending from the KwaZulu-Natal border and the Wild Coast southwestward, through Algoa Bay, to the lush evergreen Tsitsikamma park, and inland to the foothills of the Drakensberg and the semi-arid edges of the Great Karoo, offers scenic diversity and splendour. The provincial capital is the small town of Bhisho, though Port Elizabeth serves as its economic centre.*

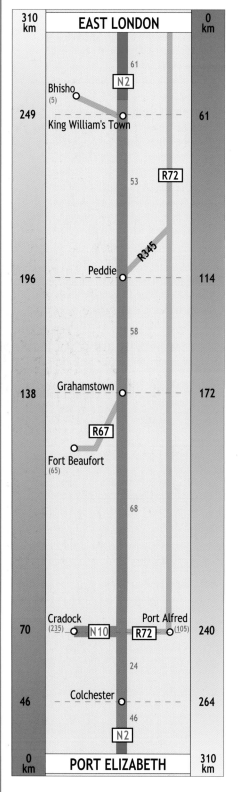

## ACCOMMODATION

**Fish River**
**Tsolwana Nature Reserve,**
tel: (043) 742-4450; three well-appointed homesteads.
**Fish River Sun Hotel,**
tel: (040) 676-1101; up-market resort.
**Hogsback**
**Hogsback Inn,** tel: (045) 962-1006; beautiful nature walks and prolific bird life.

## USEFUL CONTACTS

**Nelson Mandela Bay Tourism,** Port Elizabeth, tel: (041) 585-8884.
**Tourism Buffalo City,** East London, tel: (043) 722-6015, fax: 743-5091.
**Grahamstown Tourism Information/Makana Tourism,** tel: (046) 622-3241, fax: 622-3266.
**Automobile Association (AA),** the nationwide AA emergency rescue service number is, tel: 083 843 22.

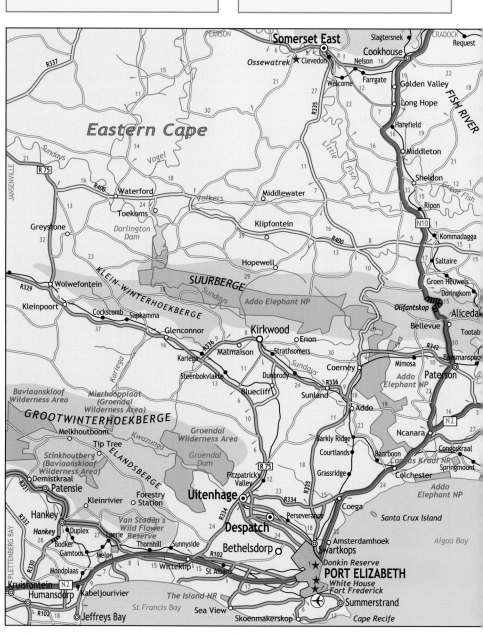

## TRAVEL TIPS

The N2 leads west to Cape Town and northeast to Durban. The R32 links Port Elizabeth with Cradock. Wild Coast resorts are accessible via subsidiary (often gravel) roads leading off the N2. When using these roads, beware of potholes, hairpin bends and straying animals.

*Right: Grahamstown is known as the 'City of Saints' for the large number of its churches and as the 'settler city' for its British-colonial origins. For an insight into South African theatre, dance, music, film, fine arts and crafts, don't miss the National Festival of the Arts held in July every year.*

## MAIN ATTRACTIONS

**Jeffreys Bay:** a surfer's paradise.
**Grahamstown:** academic and cultural centre; hosts acclaimed National Arts Festival each June/July.
**Great Fish River Conservation Area:** home to hippo, buffalo and black rhino.
**Tsolwana Game Reserve:** truly magnificent mountain reserve.
**Hogsback:** northwest of King William's Town, set among the exquisite forests which provided the inspiration for JRR Tolkien's novel, *The Hobbit*.
**Port Alfred:** pretty resort town at the mouth of the Kowie River.
**Shamwari Game Reserve:** the southernmost private big game reserve in Africa — malaria free.

Scale 1: 960 000

0    20    40 km

0    10    20 miles

N

Eastern Cape

# Port Elizabeth

*K*nown as the 'friendly city' and also as the 'windy city', Port Elizabeth is the economic hub of the Eastern Cape, much of its industrial activity revolving around the vehicle assembly sector and related enterprises. P.E., as it is most often called, is also a major tourist centre. Set on the shores of Algoa Bay, the country's fifth largest metropolis has some excellent beaches, many historic buildings, sophisticated shopping centres, good hotels and restaurants. Port Elizabeth owes its origins to the 4000 British settlers who landed here in 1820.

## MAIN ATTRACTIONS

**Beaches:** Port Elizabeth has four major beaches: King's, Humewood, Hobie and Pollok, each with its special attractions.
**Bayworld and Museum Complex:** at Humewood; see the performing dolphins and seals and visit the Aquarium and Snake Park.
**Nature rambles:** in and around P.E. lie **St Georges Park** and the **Pearson Conservatory**, **Settlers Park**, the **Island Conservation Area** and the beautifully tended **Van Stadens Wild Flower Reserve**.
**Addo Elephant National Park:** this park, located about 72km (45 miles) northeast of the city, was created in 1931 to protect the few remaining survivors of the once-prolific herds of

Cape elephant. The sanctuary offers good game-viewing and comfortable accommodation.
**Donkin Heritage Trail:** a steeply winding historical walking tour.
**Fort Frederick:** building of historical significance built in 1799; located on Belmont Terrace, overlooking the Baakens River estuary.
**Sardinia Bay:** marine reserve with miles of unspoilt coastline and crystal clear water; excellent for diving, horse riding and scenic walks or hikes.
**Boardwalk Casino and Entertainment World:** family entertainment, shopping, dining and gaming; set around a series of man-made lakes and beautiful gardens lit by 40,000 Tivoli lights.

## ACCOMMODATION

**Beach Hotel**, Humewood, tel: (041) 583-2161, fax: 583-6220; close to Bayworld and Hobie Beach.
**The Edward Hotel**, tel: (041) 586-2056, fax: 586-4925; Edwardian-style; overlooks Donkin Memorial.
**The Humewood Hotel**, Beach Road, tel: (041) 585-8961, fax: 585-1740; family hotel, attractive rooms.
**Formule 1 Hotel**, Beach Road, tel: (041) 585-6380, fax: 585-6383; budget.
**Protea Lodge**, Prospect Hill, tel/fax: (041) 585-1721; budget, Victorian comfort, self-catering.
**King's Tide Boutique Hotel:** tel: (041) 583-6023, fax: (041) 583-3389; four-star luxury with all amenities, indoor and outdoor entertainment.

## USEFUL CONTACTS

**St George's Hospital**, tel: (041) 392-6111, fax: 392-6000.
**Automobile Association**, emergency number, tel: 083 843 22.
**Computicket**, tel: 083 915 8000.

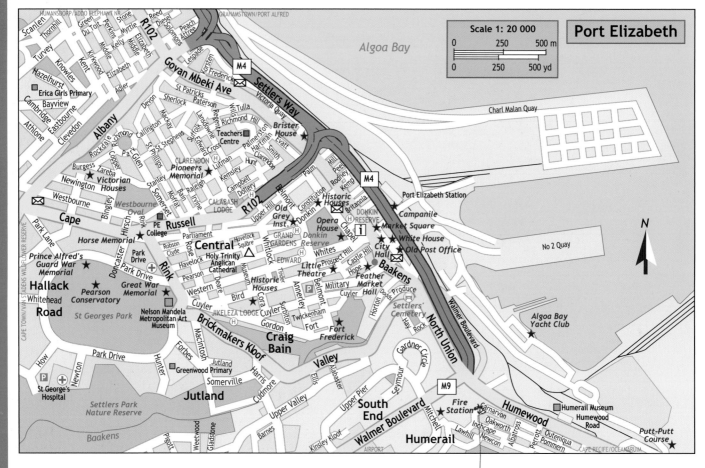

Paxton

# East London

Situated at the mouth of the Buffalo River, the river port of East London combines the charm of a relatively small community with all the essential amenities of a large city. Its attractions are of the quiet, undemanding, family-orientated kind: it has fine beaches, pleasant parks and gardens, good hotels and restaurants, and some entertaining nightlife in the summer months, especially in the seafront area. The principal thoroughfare, Oxford Street, is lined with a variety of modern shops, many of which cater to the tourist trade. The port serves the industries of the Eastern Cape and the Free State.

## ACCOMMODATION

**Blue Lagoon Hotel**, Blue Bend Place, Beacon Bay, tel: (043) 748-4821, fax: 748-2037; situated very close to the beach.

**Dolphin View Lodge**, Seaview Terrace, tel: (043) 702-8600. On the beachfront.

**Garden Court East London**, cnr John Bailey and Moore streets, tel: (043) 722-7260, fax: 743-7360; on beachfront, standard rooms, service and value.

**Kennaway Protea**, tel: (043) 722-5531; close to the city centre and the beaches, solid value.

**Premier Hotel King David**, cnr Currie Street and Inverleith Terrace, tel: (043) 722-3174. Very central.

**Windsor Cabanas and The Courtyard**, tel: (043) 743-2225; Mediterranean-style, fine views, self-catering option.

**The Thatch Guest House**, 37 Flamingo Crescent, Beacon Bay, tel: (043) 748-3672, fax: (043) 748-6227. Offers luxury and tranquility. Close to the city centre.

**Tidewaters B&B**, 1 Tidewaters Drive, Gonubie, tel: (043) 740-4505, fax: 740-5813; on Gonubie River, with spa.

## MAIN ATTRACTIONS

**Superb beaches:** most popular and accessible is Orient Beach.

**East London Museum:** Oxford Street; exhibits include the first coelacanth (hitherto thought to be extinct) to be caught and the world's only dodo egg.

**Aquarium:** over 400 species.

**Queens Park Botanical Gardens:** splendour of indigenous flora.

**Ann Bryant Gallery:** fine local paintings and sculptures.

**Hiking trails:** a choice of walks from the 4-day Shipwreck Trail to the 2-hour Umtiza Trail lead nature lovers along unspoilt beaches, through nature reserves, or into the Amatola mountains to the northwest of East London.

**Latimer's Landing:** a waterfront development on the banks of the Buffalo River. It offers a variety of restaurants overlooking the small craft anchorage where various boat and yacht rides are offered.

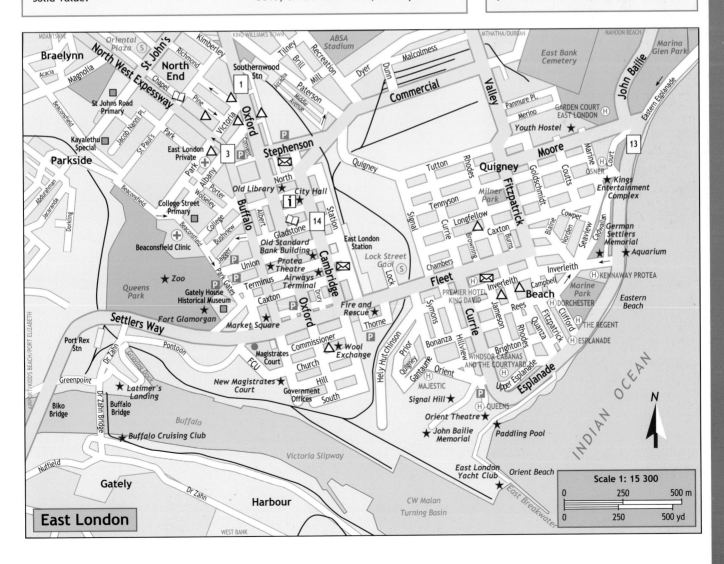

East London

# Garden Route

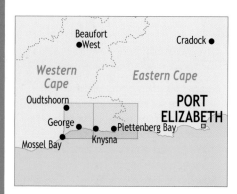

*The southern coastal terrace, extending from Humansdorp, the Tsitsikamma and Storms River in the east to Mossel Bay and beyond in the west, is known as the Garden Route. This is an enchanting shoreline of lovely bays and coves, high cliffs and wide estuaries, with a hinterland of mountains, spectacular passes, rivers, waterfalls and wooded ravines. The lagoons and lakes around Knysna and Wilderness are magical stretches of water. The attractions are many: good hotels and eating places, pleasant villages and resorts, and a warm ocean that beckons bather, yachtsman and angler alike. Inland you'll find the town of Oudtshoorn, its surrounding ostrich farms and, to the north, the magnificent Cango Caves.*

## ACCOMMODATION

**Wilderness**
**Protea Hotel Wilderness,**
tel: (044) 877-1110, fax: 877-0600;
excellent quality, set between forest and
sea. Conference facilities available.
**Fairy Knowe Hotel,**
tel: (044) 877-1100, fax: 877-0364;
on the banks of the Touw River.
**Wilderness Beach Hotel,**
tel: (044) 877-1104. Overlooks the ocean.
**Knysna**
**Brenton-on-Sea,**
tel: (044) 381-0081; 15km (9 miles)
from Knysna.

**Plettenberg Bay**
**Beacon Island Resort,**
tel: (044) 533-1120, fax: 533-3880;
smart, in a unique setting.
**Tsala Treetop Lodge,**
tel: (044) 532-7818; exclusive retreat.
**Sedgefield**
**Lake Pleasant Living,**
tel: (044) 343-1985, fax: 343-2589;
five-star hotel, superb facilities.
**Oudtshoorn**
**Protea Hotel Riempie Estate,**
tel: (044) 272-6161, fax: 272-6772;
close to Highgate Ostrich Farm.

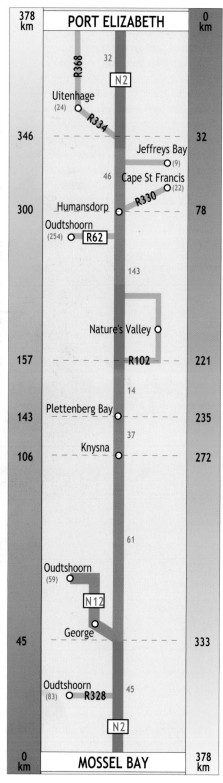

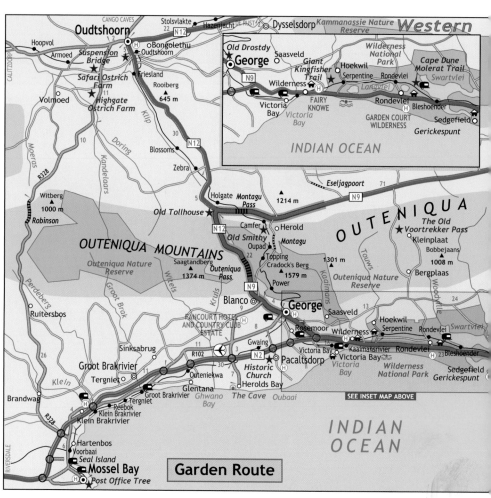

**Below:** *Hikers on the Tsitsikamma Trail, which winds its way through the park's scenic countryside. Baboon, vervet monkey, honey badger and bushpig are often encountered.*

## MAIN ATTRACTIONS

**Tsitsikamma National Park** and **Otter Trail:** an 80km (50-mile) strip of superb coastline and large offshore marine reserve.

**Storms River Mouth:** dramatic scenery at this spectacular site; spend a night in the chalets.

**Plettenberg Bay:** fashionable holiday resort with beautiful beaches.

**Mossel Bay:** excellent beaches and the Bartolomeu Dias Museum.

**Goukamma Nature Reserve:** short distance west of Knysna; unspoilt nature and wonderful bird life.

**Garden of Eden:** a beautiful forest area; many of its trees are labelled.

**Knysna:** charming little resort town with an attractive lagoon.

**Wilderness Lake Area:** superb scenery and prolific bird life.

**Oudtshoorn:** famous for its fascinating ostrich farms.

**Cango Caves:** complex of caverns ranked among the most remarkable of Africa's many natural wonders.

**Bungi jumping:** jump off Gourits River bridge or Bloukrans bridge. *See* www.faceadrenalin.com for more info.

## USEFUL CONTACTS

**Tsitsikamma National Park**, tel: (042) 281-1607, fax: 281-1843.

**Oudtshoorn Tourism Bureau**, tel: (044) 279-2532.

**Mossel Bay Tourism Bureau**, tel: (044) 691-2202.

**Plettenberg Bay Info**, tel: (044) 533-4065.

**Wilderness Tourism**, tel: (044) 877-0045.

**George Tourism Bureau**, tel: (044) 801-9295.

**Knysna Private Hospital**, tel: (044) 384-1083.

**Knysna Tourism**, tel: (044) 382-6960.

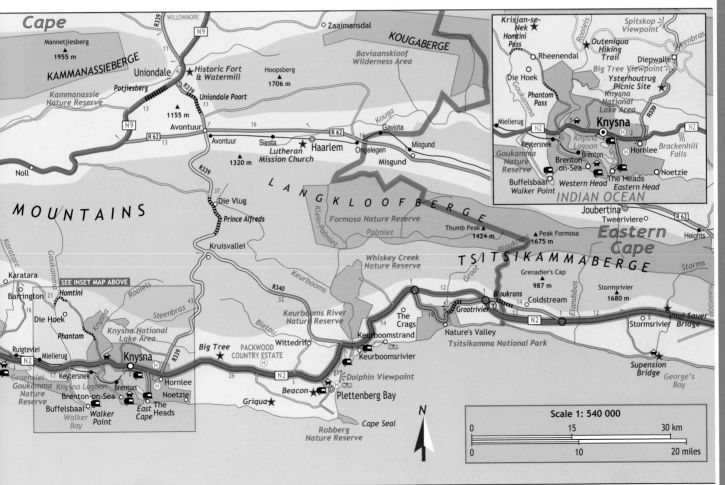

# George

*T*his pleasant little city, which was named after England's King George III, lies at the foot of the splendid Outeniqua Mountains and is the Garden Route's principal urban centre. The surrounding countryside is given over to mixed farming, forestry and the cultivation of hops. The town is linked to Knysna by the main Garden Route highway.

**Above:** *The Outeniqua Choo-Tjoe, an old steam train, offers tourists an especially scenic excursion between George and Mossel Bay.*

## ACCOMMODATION

**Fancourt Hotel and Country Club Estate**, tel: (044) 804-0000; elegant accommodation; excellent golfing.
**Oakhurst Manor House Hotel**, tel: (044) 874-7130; country-style accommodation in town.
**Far Hills Country Hotel**, tel: (044) 889-0000; country hotel overlooking the Outeniqua Mountains.

## MAIN ATTRACTIONS

**Outeniqua Choo-Tjoe:** board this old steam train for a museum-to-museum trip to Mossel Bay. This 52km (32-mile) journey offers beautiful views of the Garden Route. Tel: (044) 801-8288.
**George Museum:** in the Old Drostdy; noted for its antique musical instruments.
**Churches:** visit St Mark's, South Africa's smallest cathedral; the Dutch Reformed church, completed in 1842; and St Peter and St Paul, the oldest Roman Catholic church in the country.
**Beaches:** excellent bathing, fishing and sun-worshipping at Herold's and Victoria bays.

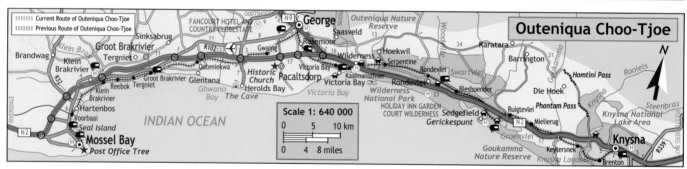

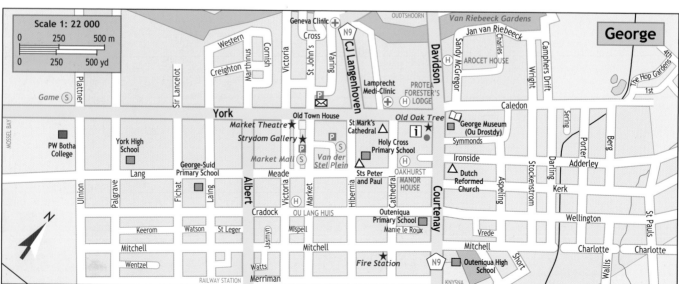

# Knysna

**K**nysna is one of the Garden Route's best-known travel destinations. Nature quite literally knocks on your front door. The town nestles on the shores of an estuary fed by rivers originating in the Outeniqua Mountains, it is surrounded by lush indigenous forests and is cooled by a sea breeze from the Indian Ocean. In and around Knysna one will find a selection of fine restaurants (the famous Knysna oyster features on many a menu), activities, cultural and heritage experiences, adventure and natural encounters to match your mood, age, physique and budget. For the shopper there are interesting outlets around every corner, including a quaint Waterfront shopping complex and authentic African traders.

## MAIN ATTRACTIONS

**Knysna Heads:** two promontories guarding the entrance to Knysna Lagoon, with good views of the surrounds.
**Royal Hotel:** Prince Alfred and George Bernard Shaw stayed here.
**Millwood Museum:** local history, gold mining and timber industry.
**Fresh oysters:** try some, sprinkled with fresh lemon juice or hot chilli sauce, at the Knysna Oyster Co.
**Crab's Creek:** a restaurant on the water's edge; sit under umbrellas and enjoy the prolific bird life.
**Noetzie:** stroll past the five castles overlooking the sea (please note that they are private residences).
**Knysna Forest:** together with the Tsitsikamma Forest, it forms the largest expanse of indigenous high forest in South Africa.
**Elephant Park:** educates all ages about the Knysna elephants, tel: (044) 532-7732, fax: 532-7763.
**Featherbed Bay Nature Reserve,** ferry ride across the bay to the lovely reserve where you can hike, picnic, or dine at the restaurant, tel: (044) 382-1693, fax: 382-2373.

## ACCOMMODATION

**Belvidere Manor**, tel: (044) 387-1055; historic home at the edge of the lagoon.
**Point Lodge**, tel: (044) 382-1944; lakeside, owner-managed, friendly, tranquil setting, *en-suite* rooms.
**Leisure Isle Lodge**, on Ballard Bay, tel: (044) 384-0462; top-rated guesthouse, superb views.
**Yellowwood Lodge**, tel: (044) 382-5906; owner-managed, friendly, beautiful *en-suite* rooms, fine views of lagoon.
**Inyathi Guest Lodges**, tel: (044) 382-7768, e-mail: info@inyathi-sa.com Individually decorated wooden chalets in the heart of Knysna set in a mostly indigenous garden. Multilingual owner.

**The Russell Hotel**, cnr Long, Unity and Graham sts, tel: (044) 382-1058; luxurious hotel centrally situated within walking distance of all Knysna's popular attractions.
**Pezula Resort Hotel**, Lagoonview Drive, Pezula Estate, tel: (044) 302-3410 (reservations); exclusive cliff-top retreat with its own golf course.
**Lightleys Holiday Houseboats,** Belvidere Off-ramp, Phantom Pass Road, N2, Belvidere/Brenton, tel: (044) 386-0007; catered or self-catered, fully equipped 2-, 4- and 6-berth boats on the safe, tranquil waters of the Knysna Lagoon. Ideal for family holidays or romantic getaways.

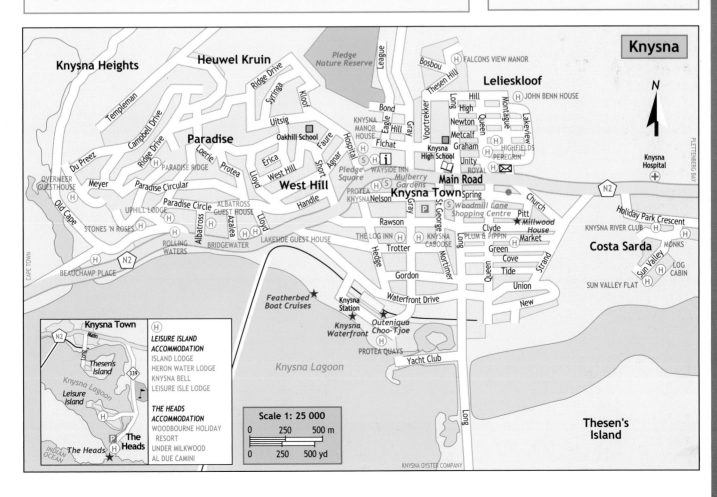

# Cape Winelands

*To the north and east of Cape Town is the Winelands, a region of grand mountain ranges, fertile valleys, vineyards and orchards, and of homesteads built in the distinctive and gracious Cape Dutch style. Among its more notable attractions are the various wine routes. Stellenbosch, the country's second oldest urban centre, is the principal town.*

## MAIN ATTRACTIONS

**Stellenbosch:** hub of the wineland region; a picturesque university town that prides itself on its lovely historic buildings and oak-lined avenues.

**Franschhoek:** founded by French Huguenots between 1680 and 1690. Protestant settlers were forbidden to form independent communities and, through intermarriage, lost much of their cultural heritage, but they left an indelible mark on the local wine-growing industry.

**Paarl:** original farming settlement established in 1720; visit a number of splendid wine estates in the vicinity of this little town.

**Somerset West:** the beautiful big homestead of Vergelegen estate was built by an early Cape governor and completed in 1701.

**Durbanville:** situated in peaceful surroundings, the wine estates offer high-quality wines.

## USEFUL CONTACTS

**Durbanville Tourism Office,**
tel: (021) 970-3172.

**Vignerons de Franschhoek** (Wine Route), tel: (021) 876-3603.

**Franschhoek Tourism Bureau,** tel: (021) 876-3603, fax: 876-2964.

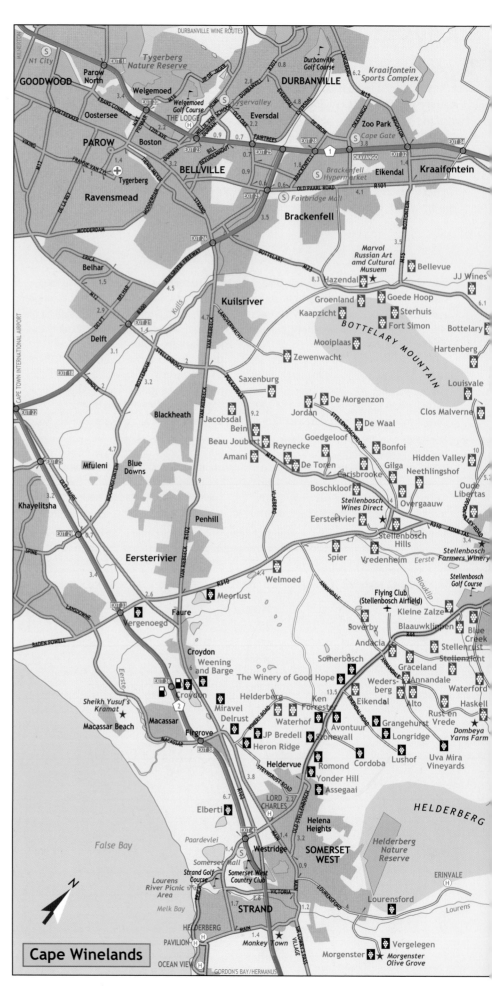

Cape Winelands

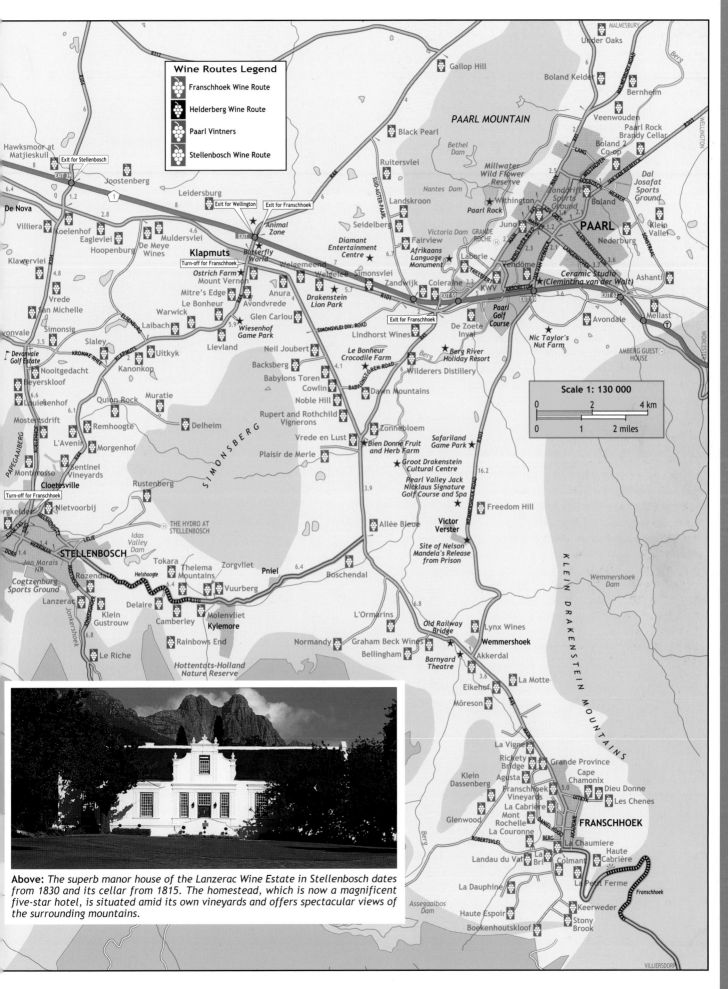

**Above:** *The superb manor house of the Lanzerac Wine Estate in Stellenbosch dates from 1830 and its cellar from 1815. The homestead, which is now a magnificent five-star hotel, is situated amid its own vineyards and offers spectacular views of the surrounding mountains.*

# Stellenbosch and Paarl

*S*tellenbosch, South Africa's second oldest urban centre and heart of the Winelands lies in a pleasant valley, less than an hour's drive from Cape Town. Founded in 1669, the settlement matured gracefully over the centuries, its broad thoroughfares lined by stately oaks and splendid historic buildings. It is the hub of an enchanting wine route and a leading seat of learning, home to a major university and several respected schools. Paarl, the biggest of the region's towns, began in 1720 as a farming and wagon-building centre, taking its name from the pearl-like cluster of granite rocks atop the overlooking mountain.

## ACCOMMODATION

**Grande Roche Hotel**, Plantasie Street, Paarl, tel: (021) 863-2727; elegant hotel with award-winning Bosman's Restaurant.

**Lanzerac Manor and Winery**, Lanzerac Road, Stellenbosch, tel: (021) 887-1132; superb facilities, elegantly refurbished; wine made on the premises.

**D'Ouwe Werf**, 30 Church Street, Stellenbosch, tel: (021) 887-4608; tradition and atmosphere combined.

**L'Auberge Rozendal**, Omega Road, Jonkershoek, tel: (021) 809-2600; on a working wine farm.

## USEFUL CONTACTS

**Stellenbosch Wine Route Office**, tel: (021) 886-4310.
**Stellenbosch Tourism and Information Bureau**, tel: (021) 883-3584, fax: 883-8017.
**Paarl Vintners**, tel: (021) 863-4886.
**Paarl Tourism Bureau**, tel: (021) 872-4842.

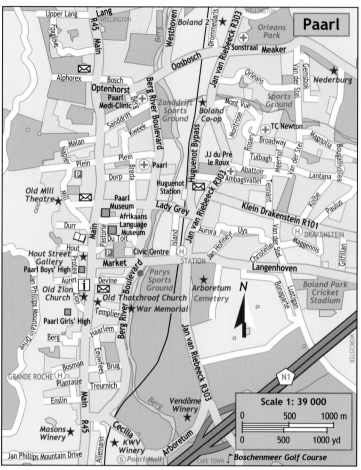

Paarl. Scale 1: 39 000

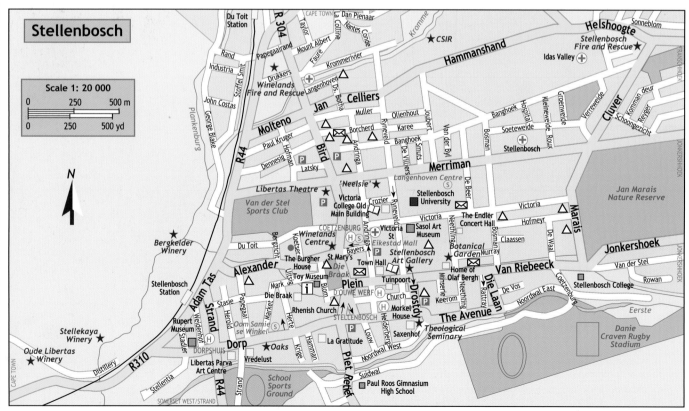

Stellenbosch. Scale 1: 20 000

# West Coast

*The western shores of the country, pounded by the cold Atlantic Ocean, are a rather barren region of low coastal vegetation. Sleepy fishing villages bake in the sun, while inland small farming communities huddle together in the vast emptiness. But the area is transformed after the spring rains, when a carpet of flowers erupts in a riot of colour stretching as far as the eye can see.*

## MAIN ATTRACTIONS

**West Coast National Park:** beautiful natural wetland reserve with prolific **bird life** and magnificent wild flowers each spring (August–October).
**Langebaan Lagoon:** a 16km-long (10-mile) inlet, the focal point of the park and a paradise for bird-watchers, anglers, and water-sports enthusiasts.
**Club Mykonos**, a splendid Greek-style leisure and accommodation complex, is located nearby.

**Above:** *After the spring rains, the parched land lies resplendent in a colourful tapestry of flowers.*

## ACCOMMODATION

**Protea Hotel Saldanha Bay,** 51B Main Street, Saldanha, tel: (022) 714-1264, fax: 714-4093.
**Lambert's Bay Hotel**, 72 Voortrekker Street, Lambert's Bay, tel: (027) 432-1126, fax: 432-1036; a comfortable and friendly establishment.

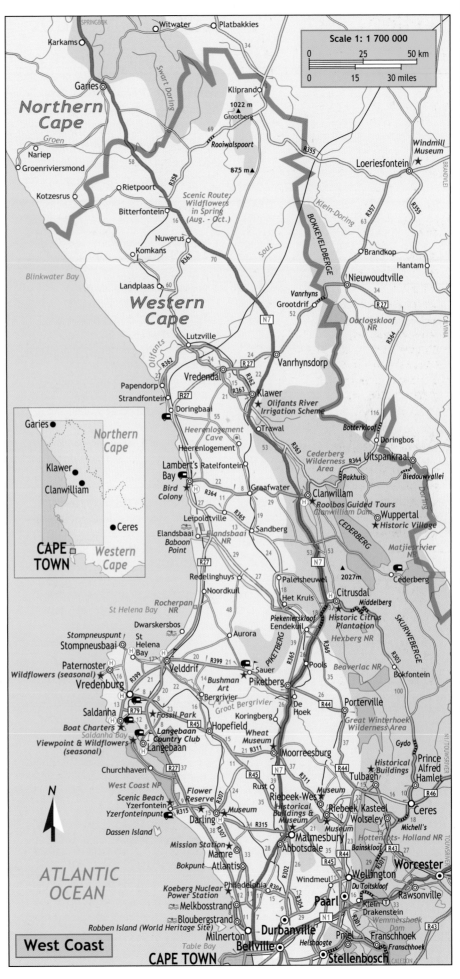

# Cape Peninsula

*The Cape Peninsula stretches from the Cape of Good Hope and Cape Point northward to Table Bay and comprises, for the most part, a strikingly beautiful plateau that achieves its loftiest and most spectacular heights in the famed Table Mountain massif overlooking Table Bay and Cape Town — a neat, bustling metropolis of handsome buildings, elegant thoroughfares and glittering shops. The Peninsula's western seaboard is scenically superb, its eastern shoreline graced by excellent beaches and attractive residential and resort centres that are a magnet for holiday-makers, scuba divers, boating enthusiasts, surfers and sun-worshippers.*

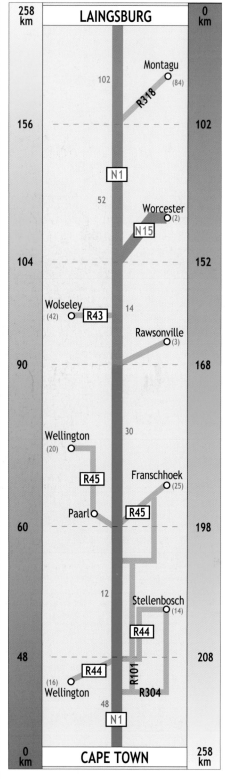

## ACCOMMODATION

**Protea Hotel Sea Point**, tel: (021) 434-3344, fax: 434-3597; comfortable accommodation.
**Peninsula All-Suite Hotel**, Sea Point, tel: (021) 430-7777, fax: 430-7776; on the promenade.
**Alphen Hotel**, tel: (021) 794-5011, fax: 794-5710; charming wine estate in Constantia Valley.
**Southern Sun Newlands Hotel**, tel: (021) 683-6562, fax: 683-6317; close to the Newlands cricket ground and rugby stadium.
**The Vineyard Hotel**, Newlands, tel: (021) 657-4500, fax: 657-4501; historic country house.
**The Lord Nelson Inn**, Simon's Town, tel: (021) 786-1386, fax: 786-1009; colonial-style inn offering old-fashioned hospitality.
**Simon's Town Quayside Hotel**, tel: (021) 786-3838, fax: 786-2241; luxury hotel, waterfront setting.
**Lord Charles Hotel**, Somerset West, tel: (021) 855-1040, fax: 855-1107; gracious elegance; world-class.

## TRAVEL TIPS

Rail, bus and taxi services are adequate. Major international car-hire companies are represented, as are local car, camper, and caravan-hire firms. Tour operators offer a wide choice of one-day and half-day scenic coach trips. Please note: metered taxis must be booked or boarded at the designated stands, as they do not cruise for fares.

**Above:** *A cable car takes visitors up to the lookout at Cape Point for panoramic views of False Bay and the southern Atlantic Ocean.*

## MAIN ATTRACTIONS

**Cape Town:** this charming metropolis is set beneath the majesty of Table Mountain. *See* page 49.
**Table Mountain:** *see* page 49.
**Kirstenbosch:** *see* page 48.
**The V&A Waterfront:** *see* page 52.
**Chapman's Peak Drive:** a world-renowned scenic route.
**Clifton:** chic suburb noted for its four magnificent beaches; popular with the trendier set.
**Hout Bay:** enchanting little suburb with a quaint fishing harbour.
**Cape Point:** southernmost tip of the Peninsula; the finest of view sites.
**Robben Island:** *see* page 53.
**Simon's Town:** the headquarters of the South African Navy, noted for its proximity to the fine beaches of Seaforth, as well as the African penguin colony at Boulders. For details, see www.simonstown.com
**Constantia Wine Estates:** five estates in the Constantia Valley: Groot and Klein Constantia, Buitenverwachting, Steenberg and Uitsig. Contact Groot Constantia for information, tel: (021) 794-5128; fax: (021) 794-1999.
**Ratanga Junction:** Africa's first full-scale theme park; family entertainment, tel: 0861 200 300.
**GrandWest Casino:** situated in Goodwood, includes gaming rooms, eateries and an olympic-size ice-rink, tel: (021) 505-7777, fax: 534-1277.

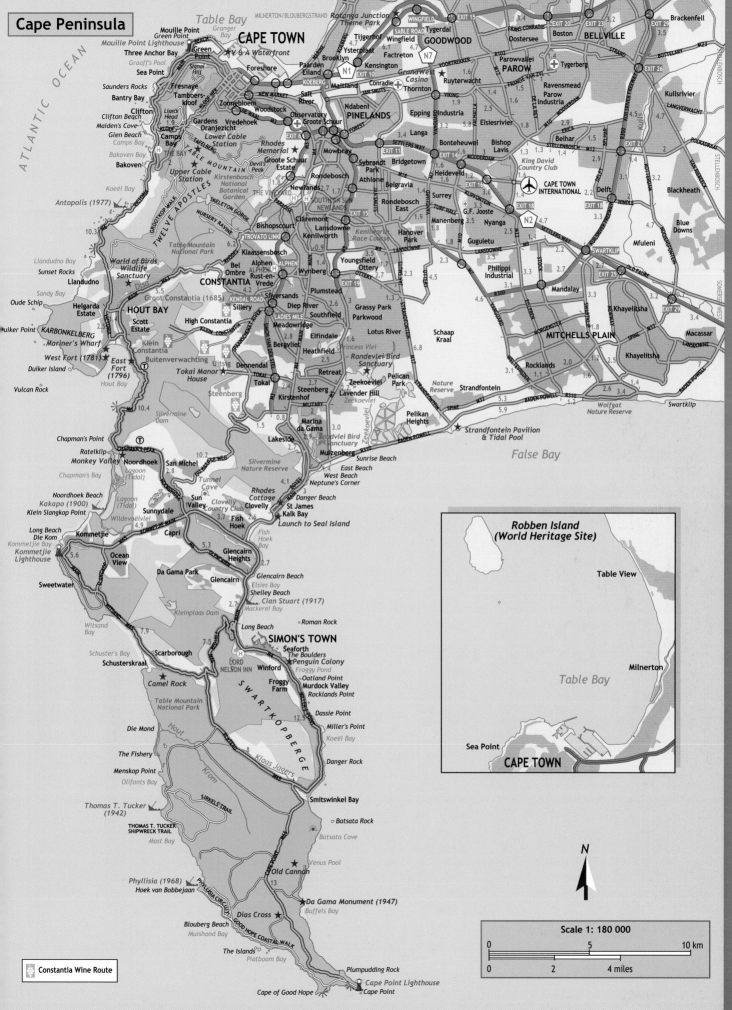

# Cape Peninsula

# Kirstenbosch

*T*he Kirstenbosch National Botanical Garden lies on the eastern slopes of the Table Mountain range. An astonishing array of flowering plants, representative of about a quarter of South Africa's 24,000 species, is cultivated here. Delightful walks lead through herb and fragrance gardens, and through stinkwood and yellowwood groves. There is a pelargonium koppie and a cycad amphitheatre, and the bird life, particularly the sunbirds drawn to the wealth of proteaceae, is enchanting. The Botanical Society Conservatory enables Kirstenbosch to display South African plants which cannot be grown in the outdoor gardens.

**Above:** *The rugged east face of the Table Mountain massif frames the delicate beauty of Kirstenbosch.*

## ENCHANTED GARDEN

**Fragrance garden:** features plants with interesting scents and textures.
**Visitors' Centre**, tel: (021) 799-8783. A glass conservatory and relaxing restaurant.
**Van Riebeeck's hedge:** part of the original wild almond hedge planted by the first Dutch settlers centuries ago.
**The Dell:** the oldest part of the garden; tree ferns and shade-loving plants.
**Sunday music concerts:** sundowner picnics in summer.
**Kirstenbosch Garden**, tel: (021) 799-8899, www.sanbi.org

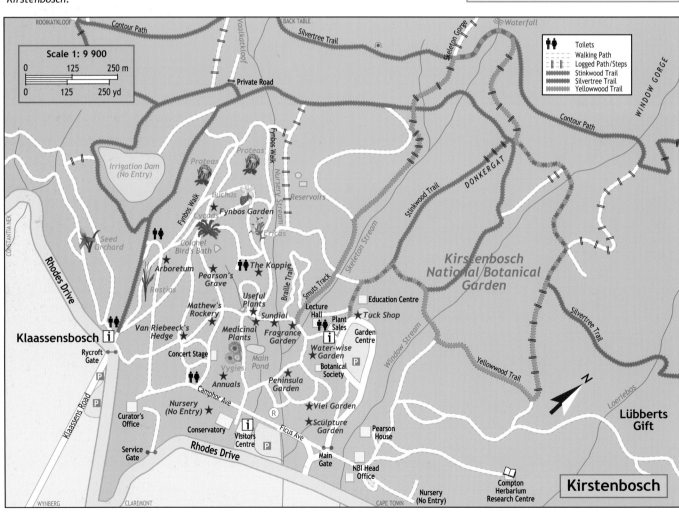

# Cape Town

*T*he central metropolitan area of Cape Town huddles in a 'bowl' formed by Table Mountain, its flanking peaks and the broad sweep of Table Bay. Founded by Dutch settlers in 1652, this is the country's oldest city and fourth largest in terms of population. More than 300 years of history have created its unique architectural character — a vibrant blend of Dutch, French, English and Malay influences. It is an attractive, colourful city that boasts excellent hotels and restaurants, open-air markets and shops catering for every pocket and taste. The central area is small, compact, and easily explored on foot.

## MAIN ATTRACTIONS

**Table Mountain:** ride the cable car or hike to the summit, and enjoy the breathtaking views.

**Castle of Good Hope:** the city's most notable edifice (built between 1666 and 1679).

**Victoria and Alfred Waterfront:** *see page 52.*

**St George's Cathedral:** visit the famous Rose Window over the south transept in this lovely church.

**Greenmarket Square:** for bargain hunting in one of Africa's prettiest little plazas. Be sure not to miss the **Old Town House** (built 1761) which contains the Michaelis collection of 17th-century Dutch and Flemish art, tel: (021) 481-3933.

**The Company Gardens:** take a walk through the lush gardens founded by Jan van Riebeeck. While here, visit the South African Museum (tel: 481-3800),

Planetarium and National Art Gallery.

**Koopmans De Wet House:** admire the beautiful antique furniture, tel: (021) 481-3935.

**Bargains:** Cape Town's informal markets are the place to shop for contemporary African art, curios, ethnic jewellery and more. Try St George's Mall, Greenmarket Square and the Kirstenbosch Craft Market.

**Rhodes Memorial:** a grandiose monument with breathtaking views, located on the eastern slopes of Devil's Peak; lovely restaurant.

**Signal Hill:** have a sundowner and enjoy the panoramic view.

**Bo-Kaap Museum:** dedicated to the Malay culture; in one of the oldest original buildings, tel: (021) 481-3939.

**Cape Town Holocaust Centre:** the only holocaust centre in Africa, tel: (021) 462-5553, fax: 462-5554.

## ACCOMMODATION

**The Bunkhouse**, 23 Antrim Road, Three Anchor Bay, tel/fax: (021) 434-5695; budget accommodation.

**The Cape Milner Hotel**, 2a Milner Rd, Tamboerskloof, tel: (021) 426-1101, fax: 426-1109; conveniently close to town.

**Cellars-Hohenort Hotel**, Constantia, tel: (021) 794-2137, fax: 794-2149; built 1693; lovely grounds; excellent restaurant.

**Southern Sun Cullinan Hotel**, Cullinan Street, tel: (021) 418-6920, fax: 418-3559; central; excellent service.

**Mount Nelson**, Gardens, tel: (021) 483-1000, fax: 483-1001; one of the world's most elegant hotels.

**Southern Sun Cape Sun**, Strand Street, tel: (021) 488-5100, fax: 423-8875; centrel; excellent restaurants.

**Park Inn**, Greenmarket Square, tel: (021) 423-2050, fax: 423-2059; charming position in the heart of town.

**Protea President Hotel**, Bantry Bay, tel: (021) 434-8111, fax: 434-9991; luxurious, exquisitely sited on a rocky seafront.

**Below:** *The arrival of the strong southeasterly wind is heralded by the appearance of the famous 'tablecloth' over Table Mountain.*

## EVENTS AND FESTIVALS

**Minstrel Carnival:** vibrant part of the **New Year** celebrations.

**Metropolitan Handicap (J&B):** horse-racing event held in **January**.

**Cape Argus Pick 'n Pay Cycle Tour:** held on the second **Sunday** of **March**.

**Two Oceans Marathon:** this popular event takes place on **Easter Saturday**.

**Mother City Queer Project:** annual gay/lesbian festival, held in **December**.

## USEFUL CONTACTS

Cape Town Tourism, tel: (021) 487-6800.

Groote Schuur Hospital, tel: (021) 404-9111.

Table Mountain Aerial Cableway Co Ltd, tel: (021) 424-8181.

Castle of Good Hope, tel: (021) 787-1249, fax: 787-1089.

**Above:** *The mood is always festive at the Victoria and Alfred Waterfront, a tourist development which is now ranked as one of South Africa's top destinations. Table Mountain provides a grand backdrop. The universal appeal ensures that its venues bustle with visitors both day and night.*

Cape Town

Scale 1: 22 000

0   250   500 m
0   250   500 yd

N

VICTORIA & ALFRED WATERFRONT
(SEE MAP ON PAGE 52 & 53)

Mouille Point

RADISSON SAS
VILLA VIA
Metropolitan Golf Course
Granger Bay
Table Bay
Breakwater
Helicopter Flights
East Pier

Beach
Green Point Stadium-Proposed 2010 Soccer World Cup Venue (Under Construction)
Fort Wynyard
New Somerset
Victoria Wharf Shopping Centre
Table Bay
No. 7 Quay
No. 2 Quay
Victoria Basin

Green Point
Green Point Track
City
Portswood
PORTSWOOD LODGE
BMW Pavilion
Victoria & Alfred Waterfront
VICTORIA & ALFRED
No. 1 Jetty
No. 4 Jetty

Weekend Market
61
PROTEA BREAKWATER LODGE
COMMODORE
Two Oceans Aquarium
Alfred Basin
CAPE GRACE
Waterfront Clocktower Precinct

Western Boulevard
PROTEA CAPE CASTLE
Hotel and Residential Marina (Under Construction)
Yacht Marina
Waterfront Residential Marina
Ben Schoeman Dock

Somerset
PROTEA VICTORIA JUNCTION
V&A Waterfront Theatre School
CITY LODGE V&A
Design Museum
Customs Gate
Duncan Dock

Schotsche Kloof
Noon Gun
ARABELLA SHERATON
SOUTHERN SUN WATERFRONT
Cape Town International Convention Centre
Coen Steytier
Table Bay Boulevard
Customs Gate
Jackson Wharf

Gold of Africa Museum
Hans Strijdom
SOUTHERN SUN CULLINAN
CAPETONIAN
Van Riebeeck Statue
Medipark
DF Malan
Heerengracht
Royal Cape Yacht Club
Small Craft Harbour
Sturrock Graving Dock
Ocean Vanguard
Berrio

Malay Quarter
Bo-Kaap Museum
Malay Museum
CAPE TOWN INN
Fountain
Artscape
FORMULA 1
Table Bay Boulevard
N1

Christiaan Barnard Memorial
Koopmans-De Wet
St George's
Southern Sun Cape Sun
Hertzog
Oswald Pirow
Foreshore (Culemborg)
Esplanade Station

62
Shortmarket
Buitengracht
Greenmarket Square
Cape Town Station
PARK INN
Civic Centre
Woodstock Station

"Blue Lodge"
Wale
Adderley
Golden Acre
Flower Market
New Market R102
Albert

Long Street Turkish Baths
Iziko Slave Lodge
St George's Cathedral
SA Cultural History Museum
Grand Parade
City Hall
2
Sir Lowry
4
Victoria Rd

Lion Gateway
Parliament
Company's Gardens
De Tuynhuys
Castle of Good Hope
Good Hope Centre
Sir Lowry
Eastern Boulevard
Trafalgar Park

Planetarium
Iziko SA Museum
3
Rust-en-Vreugd Art Gallery
Magistrates Court
District Six Museum
Oriental Plaza

Labia Theatre
National Art Gallery
Great Synagogue
Cape Town Holocaust Centre
State Archives
Zonnebloem (District Six)
Cape Peninsula University of Technology
Moravian Chapel
Walmer Estate

MOUNT NELSON
Buitenkant
Roeland
BEST WESTERN
Zonnebloem College
GARDEN COURT EASTERN BOULEVARD
N2
Eastern Boulevard

ZION APARTMENTS
GARDEN COURT DE WAAL
Mill
Gardens Shopping Centre
Cape Town Fire Station
Jutland
De Waal—M3

De Waal Park
Cape Medi-Clinic
Reservoir
Devils Peak Estate

Vredehoek

Oranjezicht

# V & A Waterfront

*After a long separation, city and harbour are once again happily reunited through the ambitious Victoria and Alfred Waterfront redevelopment scheme, a multi-billion-rand private venture that borrowed ideas from the successful harbour projects of New York, Vancouver and Sydney among others, yet retains a sparkling, lively character of its own.*

## A DIFFICULT CHOICE

**The Hildebrand:** elegant, cosy dining.
**Morton's on the Wharf:** Cajun-Creole.
**Den Anker:** top-class Belgian cuisine.
**Belthazar:** delicious seafood.
**Ocean Basket:** variety of seafood.
**Quay 4:** restaurant and tavern.

## ACCOMMODATION

**The Table Bay Hotel**, tel: (021) 406-5000, fax: 406-5977; elegant luxury; modern convenience.
**Cape Grace Hotel**, tel: (021) 410-7100, fax: 419-7622; on the West Quay, spectacular views.
**Victoria and Alfred Hotel**, tel: (021) 419-6677, fax: 419-8955; Victorian elegance alongside the Alfred Basin; great view of Table Mountain.
**Victoria Junction Hotel**, Somerset Road, Green Point, tel: (021) 418-1234, fax: 418-5678; avant-garde; loft-style Art Deco.
**City Lodge Waterfront**, tel: (021) 419-9450, fax: 419-0460; convenient location at main entrance to the Waterfront.

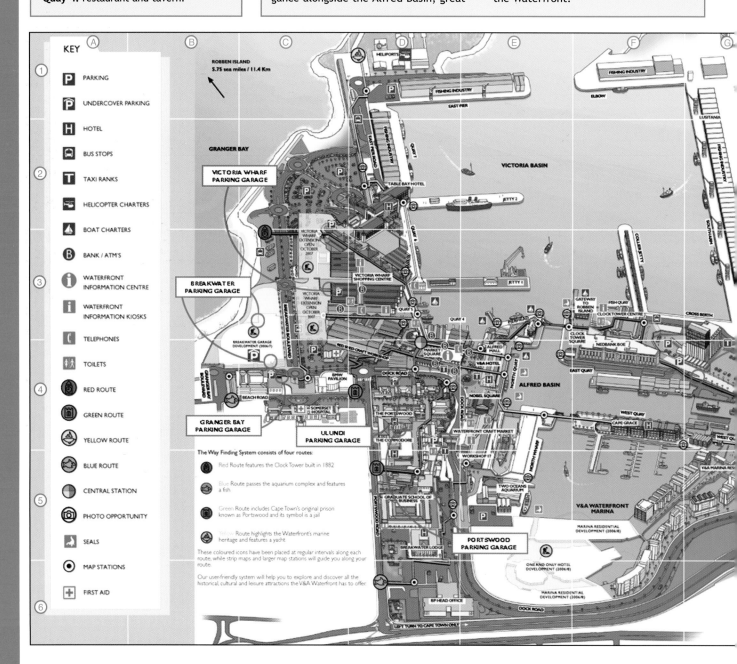

KEY

- **P** PARKING
- **P** UNDERCOVER PARKING
- **H** HOTEL
- BUS STOPS
- **T** TAXI RANKS
- HELICOPTER CHARTERS
- BOAT CHARTERS
- **B** BANK / ATM'S
- **i** WATERFRONT INFORMATION CENTRE
- **i** WATERFRONT INFORMATION KIOSKS
- TELEPHONES
- TOILETS
- RED ROUTE
- GREEN ROUTE
- YELLOW ROUTE
- BLUE ROUTE
- CENTRAL STATION
- PHOTO OPPORTUNITY
- SEALS
- MAP STATIONS
- FIRST AID

The Way Finding System consists of four routes:

- Red Route features the Clock Tower built in 1882
- Blue Route passes the aquarium complex and features a fish
- Green Route includes Cape Town's original prison known as Portswood and its symbol is a jail
- Yellow Route highlights the Waterfront's marine heritage and features a yacht

These coloured icons have been placed at regular intervals along each route, while strip maps and larger map stations will guide you along your route.

Our user-friendly system will help you to explore and discover all the historical, cultural and leisure attractions the V&A Waterfront has to offer.

## MAIN ATTRACTIONS

**Two Oceans Aquarium:** an imaginative 35 million-rand complex of world-class standard; watch shoals of fish swim through giant aquariums and explore the touch pools.

**Iziko South African Maritime Museum:** on 4000m² (13,123ft²); the largest display of model ships in South Africa. There is also a discovery cove for the children.

**SAS *Somerset*:** explore this interesting floating exhibit.

**Art and Craft Market:** filled with an enormous variety of goods that will appeal to both young and old.

**The *Victoria*:** a floating treasure museum that exhibits artefacts salvaged from ships wrecked along the coast of the Cape of Storms.

**The King's Warehouse:** sample the fare of the many diverse food stalls and shop at the huge fish market.

**The Red Shed:** watch artists at work as they create a variety of items, from delicate glass-blown flowers to colourful ethnic oil paintings and wooden toys.

**Cape fur seals:** a thriving, wild community of these mammals frequents the calm harbour waters. Watch them diving, lazily floating around, or basking in the sun.

**Boat trips:** a number of boats and smaller vessels are available for harbour and sunset cruises, as well as longer trips to historic **Robben Island**, the former prison enclave whose most famous inmate was Nelson Mandela.

**Concerts:** often held at the Amphitheatre; an event calendar is available from information kiosks.

**Shops and restaurants:** plenty of options to choose from with 400 shops, 70 eateries and extended opening hours.

**Spring Flower Show:** landscaping, gardening and flower exhibition, flower carpet, show gardens, floral art displays, a photographic exhibition and a Flower Power Concert; from 3 to 7 September.

**Air Charters & Tours, The Hopper:** NAC Makana Aviation offer Cape Town's only helicopter experience with single seats. Flights depart from the Waterfront; includes spectacular views of the city, Robben Island, Lion's Head, Table Mountain and surrounds. www.waterfront.co.za

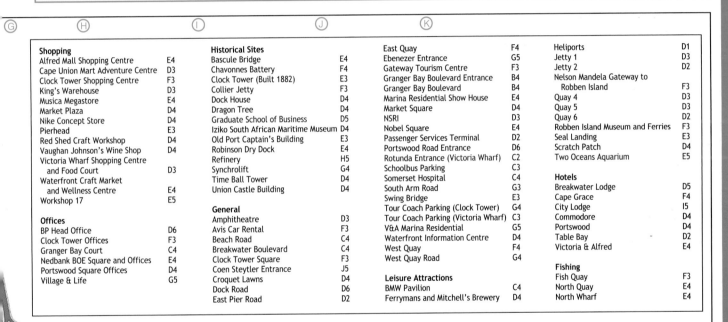

**Shopping**
| | |
|---|---|
| Alfred Mall Shopping Centre | E4 |
| Cape Union Mart Adventure Centre | D3 |
| Clock Tower Shopping Centre | F3 |
| King's Warehouse | D3 |
| Musica Megastore | E4 |
| Market Plaza | D4 |
| Nike Concept Store | D4 |
| Pierhead | E3 |
| Red Shed Craft Workshop | D4 |
| Vaughan Johnson's Wine Shop | D4 |
| Victoria Wharf Shopping Centre and Food Court | D3 |
| Waterfront Craft Market and Wellness Centre | E4 |
| Workshop 17 | E5 |

**Offices**
| | |
|---|---|
| BP Head Office | D6 |
| Clock Tower Offices | F3 |
| Granger Bay Court | C4 |
| Nedbank BOE Square and Offices | E4 |
| Portswood Square Offices | D4 |
| Village & Life | G5 |

**Historical Sites**
| | |
|---|---|
| Bascule Bridge | E4 |
| Chavonnes Battery | F4 |
| Clock Tower (Built 1882) | E3 |
| Collier Jetty | F3 |
| Dock House | D4 |
| Dragon Tree | D4 |
| Graduate School of Business | D5 |
| Iziko South African Maritime Museum | D4 |
| Old Port Captain's Building | E3 |
| Robinson Dry Dock | E4 |
| Refinery | H5 |
| Synchrolift | G4 |
| Time Ball Tower | D4 |
| Union Castle Building | D4 |

**General**
| | |
|---|---|
| Amphitheatre | D3 |
| Avis Car Rental | F3 |
| Beach Road | C4 |
| Breakwater Boulevard | C4 |
| Clock Tower Square | F3 |
| Coen Steytler Entrance | J5 |
| Croquet Lawns | D4 |
| Dock Road | D6 |
| East Pier Road | D2 |

| | |
|---|---|
| East Quay | F4 |
| Ebenezer Entrance | G5 |
| Gateway Tourism Centre | F3 |
| Granger Bay Boulevard Entrance | B4 |
| Granger Bay Boulevard | B4 |
| Marina Residential Show House | E4 |
| Market Square | D4 |
| NSRI | D3 |
| Nobel Square | E4 |
| Passenger Services Terminal | D2 |
| Portswood Road Entrance | D6 |
| Rotunda Entrance (Victoria Wharf) | C2 |
| Schoolbus Parking | C3 |
| Somerset Hospital | C4 |
| South Arm Road | G3 |
| Swing Bridge | E3 |
| Tour Coach Parking (Clock Tower) | G4 |
| Tour Coach Parking (Victoria Wharf) | C3 |
| V&A Marina Residential | G5 |
| Waterfront Information Centre | D4 |
| West Quay | F4 |
| West Quay Road | G4 |

**Leisure Attractions**
| | |
|---|---|
| BMW Pavilion | C4 |
| Ferrymans and Mitchell's Brewery | D4 |

| | |
|---|---|
| Heliports | D1 |
| Jetty 1 | D3 |
| Jetty 2 | D2 |
| Nelson Mandela Gateway to Robben Island | F3 |
| Quay 4 | D3 |
| Quay 5 | D3 |
| Quay 6 | D2 |
| Robben Island Museum and Ferries | F3 |
| Seal Landing | E3 |
| Scratch Patch | D4 |
| Two Oceans Aquarium | E5 |

**Hotels**
| | |
|---|---|
| Breakwater Lodge | D5 |
| Cape Grace | F4 |
| City Lodge | I5 |
| Commodore | D4 |
| Portswood | D4 |
| Table Bay | D2 |
| Victoria & Alfred | E4 |

**Fishing**
| | |
|---|---|
| Fish Quay | F3 |
| North Quay | E4 |
| North Wharf | E4 |

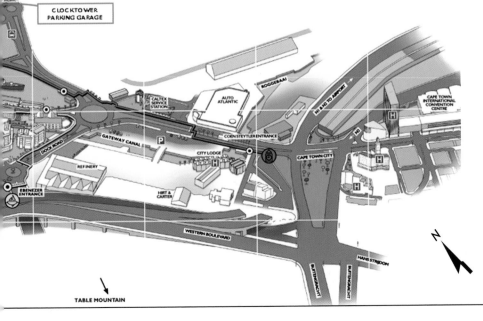

www.waterfront.co.za

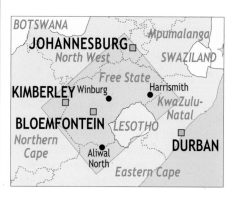

# Free State

*This rather dry, mostly flat and largely treeless east-central region of South Africa offers the visitor a number of appealing destinations, from game reserves teeming with a variety of wildlife to the evocative Bushman rock paintings along the eastern escarpment. Mine dumps greet your arrival at towns like Welkom, Allanridge and Virginia, all of which have grown up around the gold-fields that were opened up shortly after World War II.*

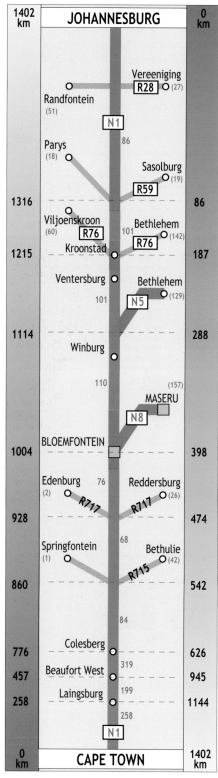

## MAIN ATTRACTIONS

**Bloemfontein:** attractive and vibrant capital of the Free State.
**Maria Moroka Nature Reserve:** a pleasant mountain reserve, near the small town of **Thaba 'Nchu** and sanctuary for antelope and other wildlife; splendid scenery.
**Golden Gate Highlands National Park:** scenic wildlife reserve with dramatically sculpted sandstone ridges and cliffs.
**The Vaal Dam:** 300km² (116-sq-mile) stretch of water, popular with boating enthusiasts and fishermen.
**Willem Pretorius Nature Reserve:** game reserve between Winburg and Ventersburg; variety of wildlife including white rhino, giraffe and buffalo; tel: (057) 651-4168.
**Gariep Dam:** the country's largest water reservoir; near Bethulie.
**Gariep Dam Nature Reserve:** located on the vast dam's northern shore; home to a very large population of graceful springbok.

## ACCOMMODATION

**Protea Hotel Black Mountain,** Groothoek Dam Rd, Thaba Nchu District, tel: (051) 871-4200, fax: 873-2521.
**Welkom Inn,** Welkom, tel: (057) 357-3361, fax: 352-1458.
**De Stijl Gariep Hotel,** Gariep Dam, tel: (051) 754-0060, fax: 754-0268.
**Hacienda Hotel,** Kroonstad, tel: (056) 212-5111, fax: 213-3298.

*Below: This visually bare landscape, near Kroonstad, is typical of the Free State. Here, a rain-laden sky dominates the great, undulating grasslands, punctuated by a solitary windmill.*

## TRAVEL TIPS

The Free State's main roads are in good condition, linking this central region with other major South African cities. Please note: distances between towns are vast, so be sure to fill up with petrol regularly.

## USEFUL CONTACTS

**Universitas Hospital,** Bloemfontein, tel: (051) 506-3500, fax: 444-5499.
**Bloemfontein Publicity Association,** tel: (051) 405-8489.
**Kimberley Information Centre,** tel: (053) 832-7298, fax: 832-7211.

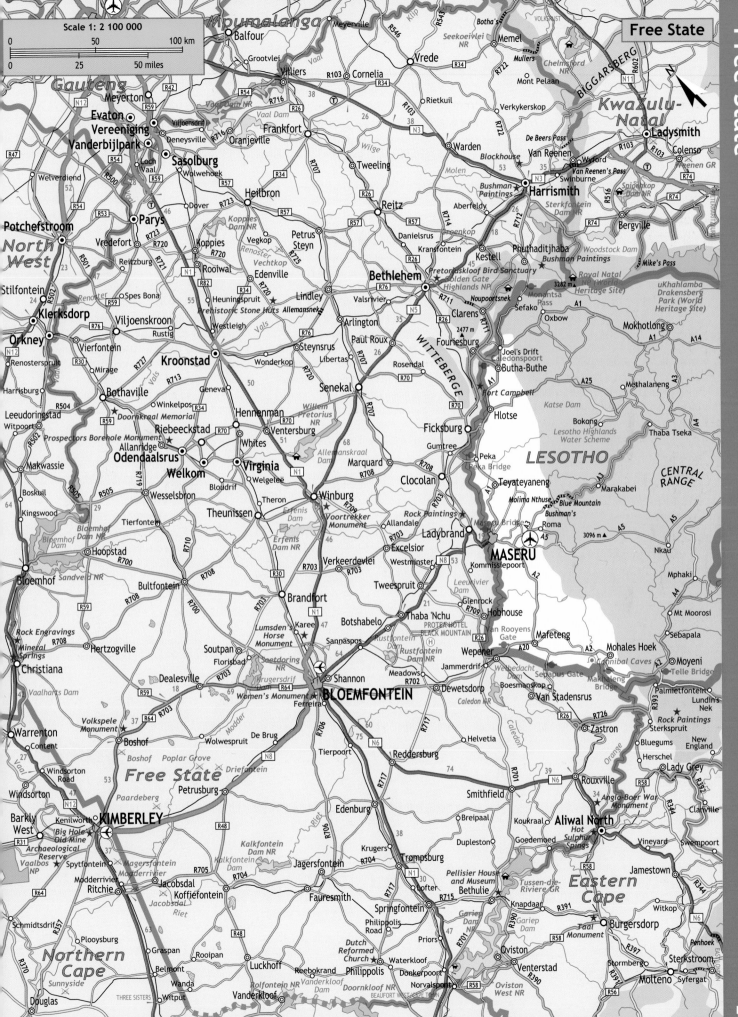

# Bloemfontein

*Bloemfontein is the judicial capital of South Africa and the principal city of the Free State. The most centrally situated of South Africa's major cities, it lies at the heart of an area of fertile farmland 1392m (4567ft) above sea level and owes much of its prosperity to the Free State goldfields, located 160km (100 miles) to the northeast. The city is noted for its impressive old buildings, museums, monuments, memorials and public parks and gardens.*

## MAIN ATTRACTIONS

**Franklin Nature Reserve:** on Naval Hill; home to a variety of wildlife.
**National Botanical Garden:** pleasant floral sanctuary dominated by impressive dolomite outcrops.
**Orchid House:** pools, waterfalls and over 3000 exquisite orchids at the foot of Naval Hill.
**The Waterfront** (Loch Logan): shops, restaurants and events.
**National Women's Memorial:** in memory of the more than 27,000 Boer women and children who died in British concentration camps during the Anglo-Boer War.

**The Old Raadsaal:** the old town hall, housed in a lovely building.
**Sand du Plessis Theatre:** modern complex; the splendid works of art contribute to the decor.
**Soetdoring Nature Reserve:** on the R64 to Kimberley; protective habitat for antelope, lion, cheetah and brown hyena.
**National Afrikaans Literary Museum:** in the Old Government Building; a treasure house of African literature, with manuscripts, etc., belonging to well-known South African writers. Also houses the Afrikaans Music Museum (musical instruments) and Theatre Museum.

## TRAVEL TIPS

Bloemfontein is on the main north-south highway, the N1, which links Cape Town to Johannesburg. Good tarred roads connect the city with all the surrounding major centres, such as Welkom (R700 and R710); Kimberley (R64); Maseru in Lesotho (R64); and East London on the coast (R30).

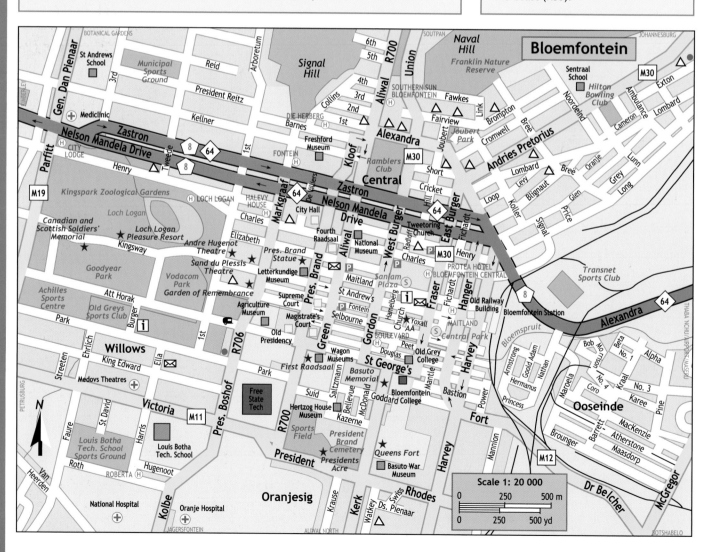

# Kimberley

*K*imberley, the world-renowned diamond centre and capital of neighbouring Northern Cape province, was born in the 1870s when tens of thousands of prospectors poured into the area to unearth the glittering gems that lay in abundance beneath the dusty ground. Kimberley still retains much of the old-world atmosphere of these heady days, when instant fortunes were made (and lost), and money and champagne flowed like water.

## ACCOMMODATION

**Garden Court Kimberley**, tel: (053) 833-1751, fax: 832-1814; lovely garden setting.
**Hotel Kimberlite**, tel: (053) 831-1968; within easy walking distance of the Big Hole.
**Horseshoe Motel**, Memorial Road, tel: (053) 832-5267.

**Right:** *When diamond fever struck in 1871, no one could have guessed that 43 years later the Big Hole would reach a depth of 1097m (3600ft). Between 1871 and 1914, 22.6 million tons of earth was excavated from the mine for a yield of 2722kg (6000lb) of diamonds.*

## MAIN ATTRACTIONS

**The Big Hole:** Kimberley's historic hub. By the time it was closed in 1914 it had yielded almost three tons of diamonds.
**Kimberley Mine Museum:** evocative and comprehensive insight into the town's lively past.
**Duggan-Cronin Gallery:** an outstanding photographic display of the San-Bushman culture.
**William Humphreys Gallery:** an excellent collection of South African and European paintings, sculpture and furniture.
**The Diggers Fountain:** honours the miners who helped to build the Diamond City.
**Magersfontein battlefield:** for directions, call tel: (053) 833-7115.
**Star of the West:** this public house was the favorite rendezvous of diamond prospectors from the early 1870s. Has a stool said to have been made specially for Cecil Rhodes.

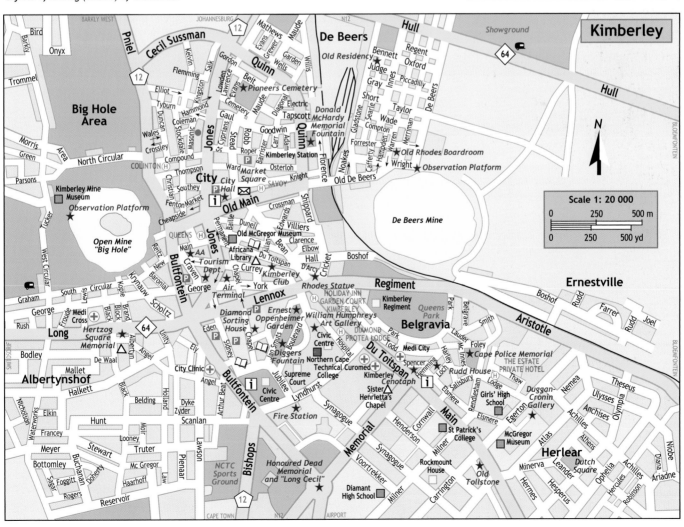

# Main Map Section Key and Legend

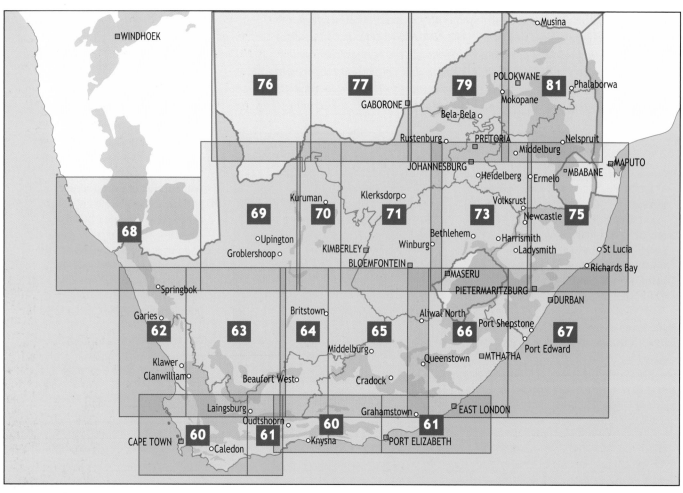

Pages 60-61
Scale 1: 1 790 000

| 0 | 50 | 100 km |
| 0 | 25 | 50 miles |

Pages 62-81
Scale 1: 1 600 000

| 0 | 50 | 100 km |
| 0 | 25 | 50 miles |

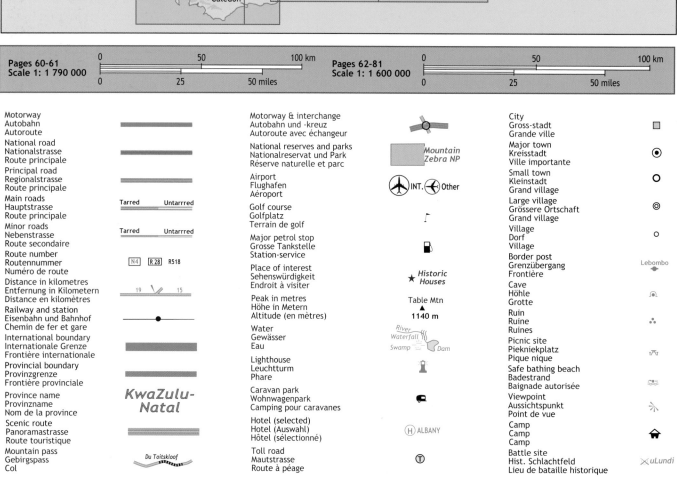

| | | | |
|---|---|---|---|
| Motorway / Autobahn / Autoroute | | Motorway & interchange / Autobahn und -kreuz / Autoroute avec échangeur | City / Gross-stadt / Grande ville |
| National road / Nationalstrasse / Route principale | | National reserves and parks / Nationalreservat und Park / Réserve naturelle et parc | Mountain Zebra NP | Major town / Kreisstadt / Ville importante |
| Principal road / Regionalstrasse / Route principale | | Airport / Flughafen / Aéroport | INT. / Other | Small town / Kleinstadt / Grand village |
| Main roads / Hauptstrasse / Route principale | Tarred  Untarrred | Golf course / Golfplatz / Terrain de golf | Large village / Grössere Ortschaft / Grand village |
| Minor roads / Nebenstrasse / Route secondaire | Tarred  Untarrred | Major petrol stop / Grosse Tankstelle / Station-service | Village / Dorf / Village |
| Route number / Routennummer / Numéro de route | N4  R28  R518 | Place of interest / Sehenswürdigkeit / Endroit à visiter | Border post / Grenzübergang / Frontière | Lebombo |
| Distance in kilometres / Entfernung in Kilometern / Distance en kilomètres | 19 \\ 15 | Peak in metres / Höhe in Metern / Altitude (en mètres) | Table Mtn ▲ 1140 m | Cave / Höhle / Grotte |
| Railway and station / Eisenbahn und Bahnhof / Chemin de fer et gare | | Water / Gewässer / Eau | River Waterfall Swamp Dam | Ruin / Ruine / Ruines |
| International boundary / Internationale Grenze / Frontière internationale | | Lighthouse / Leuchtturm / Phare | Picnic site / Piekniekplatz / Pique nique |
| Provincial boundary / Provinzgrenze / Frontière provinciale | | Caravan park / Wohnwagenpark / Camping pour caravanes | Safe bathing beach / Badestrand / Baignade autorisée |
| Province name / Provinzname / Nom de la province | KwaZulu-Natal | Hotel (selected) / Hotel (Auswahl) / Hôtel (sélectionné) | H ALBANY | Viewpoint / Aussichtspunkt / Point de vue |
| Scenic route / Panoramastrasse / Route touristique | | Toll road / Mautstrasse / Route à péage | T | Camp / Camp / Camp |
| Mountain pass / Gebirgspass / Col | Du Toitskloof | | | Battle site / Hist. Schlachtfeld / Lieu de bataille historique | uLundi |

# Eastern and Western Cape

Dominated by series after series of soaring mountain ranges interspersed with rolling wheat fields, orchards and vineyards, the southern part of South Africa is one of the continent's most beautiful regions. Inland there are forests, deep fertile valleys and spectacular mountain passes to explore, while the rugged, rocky coastline offers the visitor countless venues for safe bathing, surfing, beachcombing and fishing, together with a number of delightful holiday villages and towns. So gloriously abundant is the flora of this particular stretch of South African coastline that it has been named the Garden Route.

## MAIN ATTRACTIONS

**Wineland towns:** wide, tree-lined avenues and historic buildings.
**Day drives:** along the southern coastline; two are particularly recommended: from Cape Town to the little town of Hermanus, haven for southern right whales; and from Cape Town to Langebaan Lagoon on the West Coast, renowned for its bird life.
**The Garden Route:** from Mossel Bay to the Storms River, scenically one of the

most splendid parts of the South African coastline; visit the towns of Knysna and Plettenberg Bay.
**Hex River Valley:** dramatic sandstone crags dominate the green, beautiful valley, where excellent grapes are cultivated.
**The Klein Karoo:** a beautiful and rugged region lying between the southern coastal rampart and the Swartberg uplands to the north.

## TRAVEL TIPS

The N2 national route leads eastward along the south coast from Cape Town to East London, and is the best way to see the beautiful South African countryside. The road is wide and in excellent condition and petrol stations are frequent.

Below: A myriad vineyards have been established in the fertile soils of the beautiful Hex River Valley.

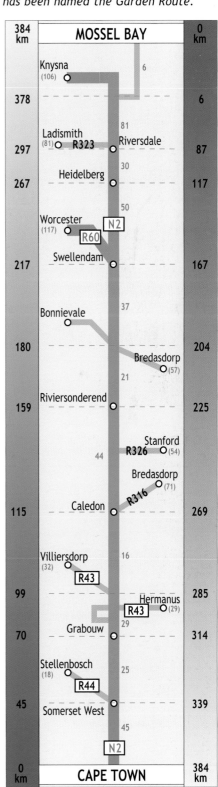

59

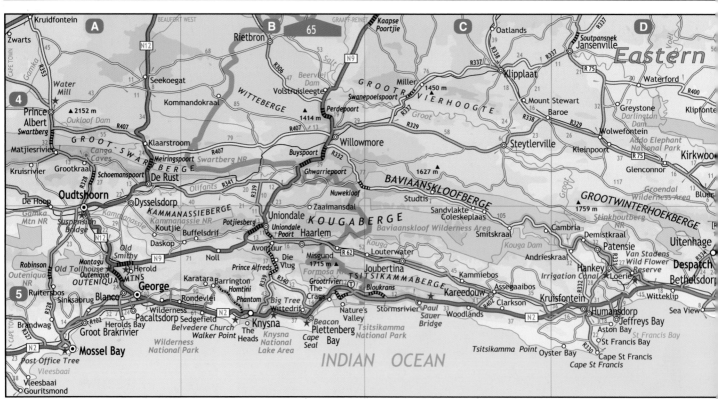

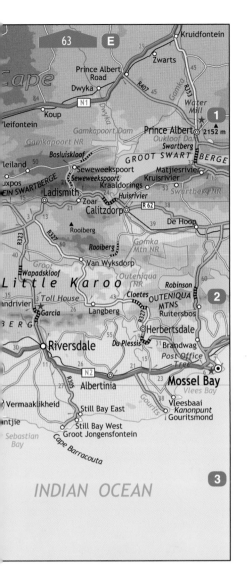

**Map E / 63 region**

Kruidfontein
Zwarts
Prince Albert Road
Dwyka
Koup
Prince Albert ▲ 2152 m
Water Mill
1
Gamkapoort Dam
Oukloof Dam
Gamkapoort NR
Swartberg
GROOT SWART BERGE
Bosluiskloof
Seweweekspoort
Matjiesrivier
Seweweekspoort
Kruisrivier
Kraaldorings
Ladismith
Zoar
Huisrivier
Swartberg NR
Calitzdorp
R 62
De Hoop
Rooiberg
Rooiberg
Gamka Mtn NR
Van Wyksdorp
Little Karoo
Wapadskloof
Robinson NR
OUTENIQUA MTNS
Cloetes
Toll House
Ruitersbos
Garcia
Langberg
Herbertsdale
Riversdale
Du Plessis
Brandwag
N2
Post Office Tree
Albertinia
Mossel Bay
Vlees Bay
Vermaaklikheid
Still Bay East
Vleesbaai
Kanonpunt
Gouritsmond
Still Bay West
Groot Jongensfontein
Sebastian Bay
Cape Barracouta
2
3
INDIAN OCEAN

**Above:** *The scenic splendour of Knysna Lagoon has ensured the resort town's popularity, and the lagoon is lined with many attractive homes and holiday retreats in garden settings.*

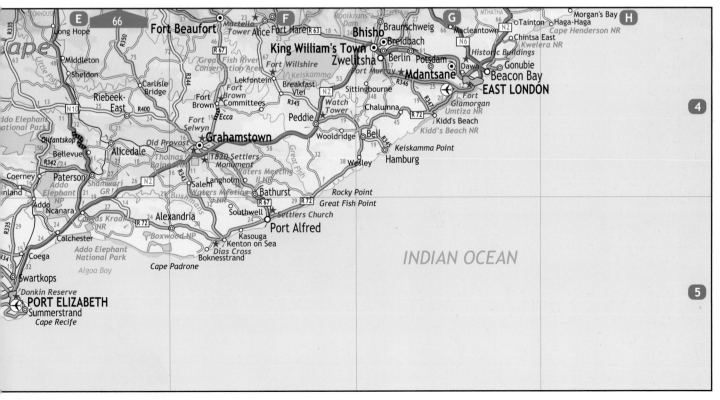

**Map E / 66 region**

Long Hope
Fort Beaufort
Martello Tower
Alice
Fort Hare
R 63
Rooikrans Dam
Braunschweig
Tainton
Haga-Haga
Morgan's Bay
Cape Henderson NR
Bhisho
Macleantown
Chintsa East
Kwelera NR
Middleton
King William's Town
Breidbach
Sheldon
Zwelitsha
Berlin
Potsdam
Historic Buildings
Carlisle Bridge
Fort Willshire
Fort Murray
Mdantsane
Dawn
Gonubie
Riebeek-East
Lekfontein
Breakfast Vlei
N2
Sittingbourne
R346
Beacon Bay
EAST LONDON
Fort Brown
Committees
R345
Chalumna
Fort Glamorgan
Umtiza NR
Olifantskop
Ecca
Peddie
R 72
Kidd's Beach
Bellevue
Fort Selwyn
Grahamstown
Wooldridge
Bell
Kidd's Beach NR
Alicedale
Old Provost
1820 Settlers Monument
Wesley
Keiskamma Point
Hamburg
Paterson
Salem
Langholm
Waters Meeting
Addo Elephant NP
Ncanara
Alexandria
Southwell
Bathurst
Rocky Point
Great Fish Point
Colchester
Kasouga
Port Alfred
Kenton on Sea
Dias Cross
Boknesstrand
Cape Padrone
INDIAN OCEAN
Coega
Addo Elephant National Park
Algoa Bay
Swartkops
Donkin Reserve
PORT ELIZABETH
Summerstrand
Cape Recife
4
5

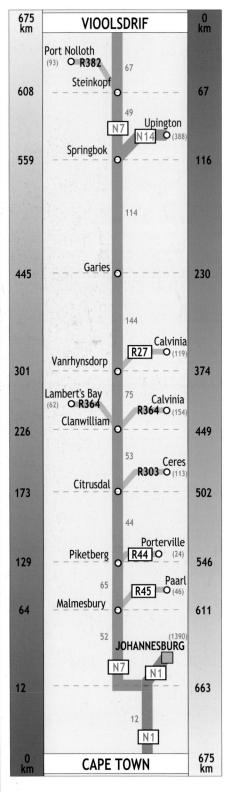

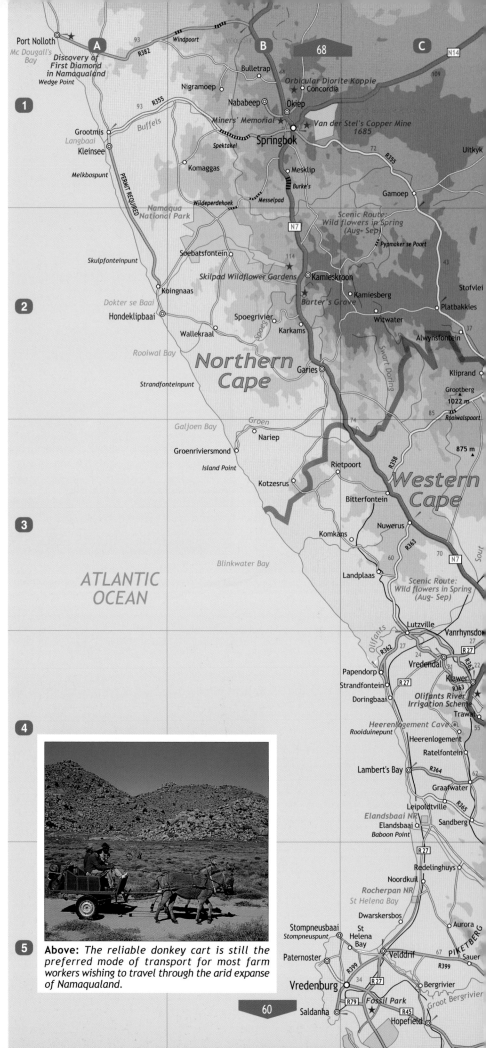

**Above:** *The reliable donkey cart is still the preferred mode of transport for most farm workers wishing to travel through the arid expanse of Namaqualand.*

D
Bloemhoek
R358

E
Bossiekom
69
Tuins

F
R27
Jaght Drift
Rooiberg Dam

G

1

Geelvloer
Karlvloer
148
Bosduiflaagte
148
Diemansputs

Granaatboskolk
Kareeboschkolk
Grootvloer
Verneuk Pan
R357

Halfweg
Zwartkop
Van Wyksvlei

R358
Katkop
Onderstedorings
Van Wyksvlei Dam
2

Konnes se Pan
Dwaggasoutpan
Rietfontein se Pan
R357
Brandvlei
149
R361
82

Commissioner's Salt Pan
R27
Northern Cape
R361

Krom
Rock Paintings ★
Swartkolk-vloer
R353
Riet se Vloer

121
R357
Blomberg se Vloer
R27

Loeriesfontein
Windmill Museum
Sakrivier
Corbelled Houses ★
Carnarvon

R355
90
Tontelbos
173
R63
Blounek

Klein-Doring
R357
R355
Sak
135
Sterling

63
89
Kootjieskolk
Williston
R63

Brandkop
Hantam
Vlakhoeksberg ▲ 1530 m
120
R353
3

Bokkeveldberge
Nieuwoudtville
HANTAMSBERG
Calvinia
GREAT KAROO
64

Vanrhyns
69
R27
Riet
Brak

Grootdrif
R27
Oorlogskloof NR Oorlogskloof
R354
93
Quaggasfontein Poort
R353
103
R356

43
R364
Bloukrans
Fish
Bonekraal
Riet
Saaifontein

Botterkloof
166
Middelpos
134
BASTERSBERGE
Corbelled House ★
Fraserburg

Doringbos
Die Bos
★ Rock Paintings
Snyderspoort
R358
4

R363
R364
Pakhuis
Biedouwvallei
ROGGEVELDBERGE
Renoster
113
Hondefontein
Teekloof
NUWEVELDBERGE

Clanwilliam
Clanwilliam Dam
Uitspankraal
1735 m ▲
R354
1913 m ▲

CEDERBERG
Wuppertal
Cederberg Wilderness Area
Tankwa-Karoo National Park
The South African Astronomical Observatory ★
Rooipoort
114
R357

53
Sneeuberg
Cederberg
Tweefontein
Sutherland
R356
Bloupoort

N7
▲ 2027 m
Doring
Bo-Wadrif
Rooikloof
Leeugamka Dam

Citrusdal
Middelberg
Rooikloof
1721 m ▲
Merweville
N1

Piekenierskloof
Matjiesrivier NR
Verlatekloof
Komsberg
SKURWEBERGE
KOMSBERGE

Eendekuil
Hoogberg NR
110
Leeu-Gamka
Kruidfontein
39
N1

47
R303
SWARTRUGGENS
121
Koringplaas
Buffels
Prince Albert Road
Zwarts
45

Pools
Bokfontein
Dwyka
R409
45

Piketberg
De Hoek
R44
Porterville
Great Winterhoek Wilderness Area
Western Cape
60
Hillandale
CAPE TOWN
84
Koup
R355
Gamka
5

27

Great Karoo

# Great Karoo

This semi-arid region of bone-dry air, minimal rainfall and intense sunshine dominates the Cape interior. The countryside stretches endlessly to the distant horizons, dotted with lonely windmills and isolated farmsteads.

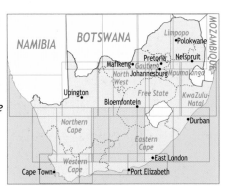

## MAIN ATTRACTIONS

**Beaufort West:** birthplace of the famed heart surgeon Chris Barnard; this little town is also noted for its lovely pear-tree-lined streets.

**Karoo National Park:** north of Beaufort West; wildlife includes mountain zebra, shy leopard and antelope.

**Graaff-Reinet:** third oldest town in the Cape, with some fine old architecture.

**Valley of Desolation:** near Graaff-Reinet; a fantasia of wind-eroded, strangely shaped dolerite peaks, pillars and balancing rocks.

**Nieu-Bethesda:** tiny hamlet, 50km (31 miles) north of Graaff-Reinet; home to the Owl House Museum's bizarre sculptures, many of which are decorated with ground glass.

**Cradock:** in the vicinity are the Mountain Zebra National Park and author Olive Schreiner's grave.

**Aliwal North:** this pleasant town to the far east of the Great Karoo has hot sulphur springs and an excellent spa.

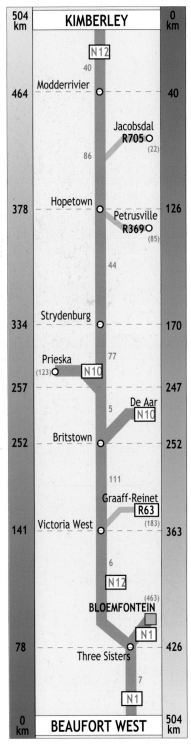

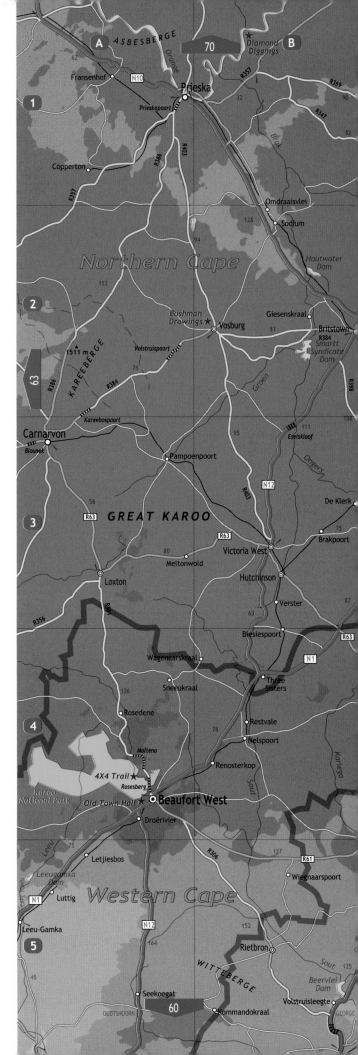

Redcliffe
Rosetta ESTCOURT
Kamberg
Nottingham Road
uKhahlamba
Drakensberg Park
(World Heritage
Site)
iMpendle
Lidgetton
Howick
Hilton
Edendale
PIETERMARITZBURG
Thornville
Bulwer
Mpumalanga
Richmond
Donnybrook
Roseland
Creighton
Bush Reserve
Riverside
iXopo
CJ Rhodes' House
Kingsburgh
Umzimkulu
Highflats
Vernon
Crookes NR
uMzinto
Stafford's Post
Bisi
Braemar
Bontrand
St Faith's
Harding
KwaDweshula
Weza
Oribi
Gorge NR
Hibberdene
Marburg
Sea Park
Bizana
Paddock
uMtentweni
Port Shepstone
Redoubt
uVongo
Margate
Munster
Ramsgate
Umtamvuna
NR
Southbroom
Banner
Rest
Glenmore Beach
Port Edward
Impisi
Umtentu
Mkambati Nature Reserve
Mkambati
South Sand Bluff
Port Grosvenor
Mbotyi

New Hanover
Dalton
Mpolweni
VALLEY OF 1000 HILLS
Ndwedwe
Tongaat
iNanda
Krantzkloof NR
Hammarsdale
Pinetown
Queensburgh
uMlazi
iSipingo
uMbogintwini
aManzimtoti
uMgababa
uMkomaas
Scottburgh
Park Rynie
Sezela
Mtwalume

75
KwaDukuza (Stanger)
Shakaskraal
Groutville
Shaka's Memorial
Salt Rock
Shaka's Rock
Ballito
Verulam
uMhlanga
KwaMashu
DURBAN
The Bluff

Tugela Mouth
Darnall
Ultimatum Tree
Fort Pearson
Blythdale Beach

KwaZulu-Natal

INDIAN OCEAN

NAMIBIA
BOTSWANA
MOZAMBIQUE
Limpopo
Polokwane
Pretoria
Nelspruit
Mafikeng
Gauteng
North West
Johannesburg
Mpumalanga
Upington
Free State
KwaZulu-Natal
Bloemfontein
Durban
Northern Cape
Eastern Cape
East London
Western Cape
Cape Town
Port Elizabeth

**Above:** *The wide mouth of the Mgeni River, in Durban, is spanned by several bridges. The renowned Mgeni River Bird Park, which houses some 300 exotic and local species and is rated the third best in the world, is accessible via the Mgeni River Bridge from the Marine Parade.*

A   B   C   D
1
2
3
4
5

# Northern Cape

*M*uch of this region — the western part — is a dry, rather forbidding moonscape of low mountains and strange plants like the kokerboom. After the rainy season, however, the arid veld is transformed into a riot of colour as wild flowers bloom in abundance. Towns are few and small, with the exception of Upington, which is beautifully situated along the banks of the Orange River.

## TRAVEL TIPS

The main highways that service the northern and northwestern Cape, and those which traverse the vast Karoo region, are generally in good condition. Note: be sure to stop for petrol and refreshments in good time, as the towns (and the service stations) tend to lie rather far apart in this region. Beware of wild animals crossing the road, especially at dawn, dusk and at night.

## MAIN ATTRACTIONS

**Upington:** visit one of the dried fruit co-ops around the town.
**Augrabies Falls National Park:** marvel at the lovely waterfall (one of the five biggest in the world) in this otherwise harsh area, and drive through the reserve to spot the bird- and wildlife.
**Kgalagadi Transfrontier National Park:** straddles the South Africa-Botswana border north of Upington. This is the first of Africa's 'peace parks'. The red sand dunes of the southern segment, shy Kalahari lion, an

abundance of raptor species, and magnificent sunsets attract nature lovers to this unique desert park.
**Goegap Nature Reserve:** east of Springbok; spot eland, springbok and mountain zebra along hiking trails and game drives.
**Richtersveld National Park:** in the far northwestern corner of the province; hauntingly beautiful.
**Vioolsdrif/Noordoewer:** South Africa-Namibia border post, for travellers heading to Namibia.

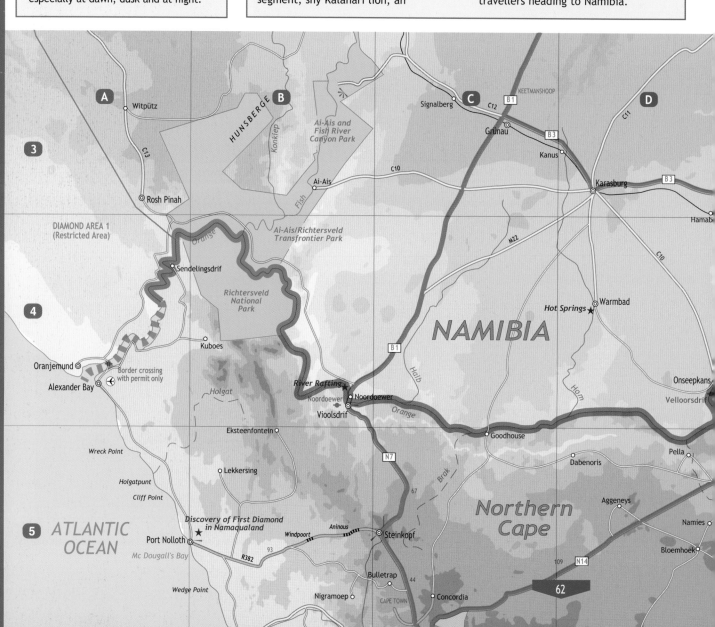

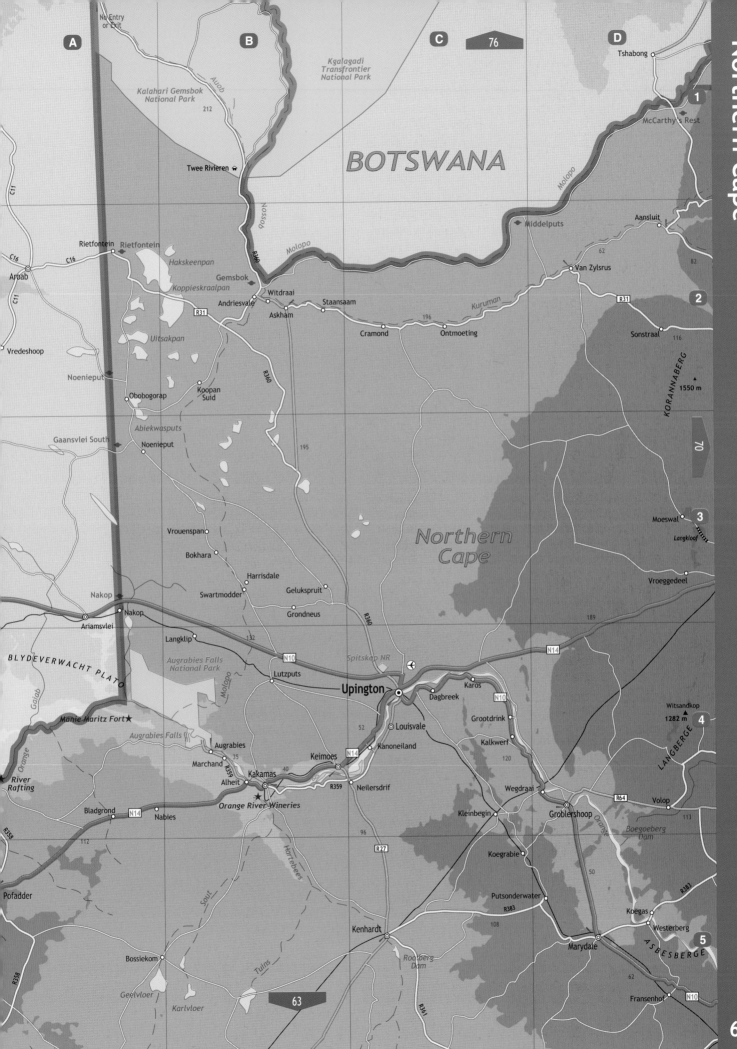

BOTSWANA

Kgalagadi
Transfrontier
National Park

Kalahari Gemsbok
National Park 212

Northern
Cape

**A** No Entry
or Exit

**B**

**C** 76

**D**

Tshabong

1

McCarthy's Rest

Middelputs

Aansluit

Van Zylsrus

82

R31

2

Auob

Nossob

Molopo

Molopo

Twee Rivieren

C11

C16

Rietfontein  Rietfontein

Aroab

C16

C11

Hakskeenpan

Gemsbok

Koppieskraalpan

Witdraai

Andriesvale

Askham

Staansaam

Kuruman

Cramond

Ontmoeting

196

Sonstraal

116

Vredeshoop

Uitsakpan

R31

KORANNABERG

1550 m

70

Noenieput

Obobogorap

Koopan
Suid

R360

Abiekwasputs

Gaansvlei South

Noenieput

195

Moeswal

3

Langkloof

Vrouenspan

Bokhara

Vroeggedeel

Harrisdale

Swartmodder

Gelukspruit

Grondneus

R360

189

Nakop

Nakop

Ariamsvlei

132

Langklip

N10

Spitskop NR

N14

N14

Louisvale

52

River
Rafting

Orange

Gaiab

BLYDEVERWACHT PLATO

Augrabies Falls
National Park

Molopo

Lutzputs

Upington

Karos

Dagbreek

N10

Grootdrink

Kalkwerf

120

Witsandkop
1282 m

4

LANGBERGE

Manie Maritz Fort ★

Augrabies Falls

Augrabies

Marchand

R359

Kakamas

Alheit

Orange River Wineries

Keimoes

N14

Kanoneiland

R359

Neilersdrif

Wegdraai

R64

Volop

Groblershoop

113

Kleinbegin

Boegoeberg
Dam

Orange

35

40

96

Bladgrond

N14

Nabies

R358

112

R27

Sout

Horrebees

Koegrabie

Putsonderwater

R383

50

R383

Koegas

Pofadder

Bossiekom

Tuins

Kenhardt

108

Marydale

Westerberg

5

ASBESBERGE

Geelvloer

Karkvloer

Rooiberg
Dam

63

R361

Fransenhof

N10

62

R358

# Kimberley and Bloemfontein

*T*hese neighbouring towns, the capitals of the Northern Cape and Free State provinces respectively, are situated on the high interior plateau. Both offer fine museums and sandstone buildings of historical interest and are surrounded by nature reserves and dams.

**Above:** *The statue of Christiaan Rudolph de Wet stands in front of Bloemfontein's Fourth Raadsaal, the last government seat of the old Republic.*
**Below:** *The Kimberley Mine Museum portrays life on the diamond fields more than a century ago.*

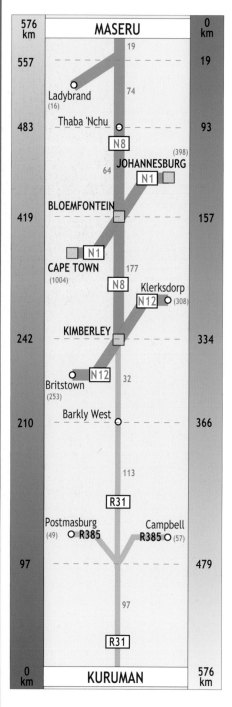

| 576 km | MASERU | 0 km |
|---|---|---|
| | 19 | |
| 557 | | 19 |
| | 74 | |
| Ladybrand (16) | | |
| 483 | Thaba 'Nchu | 93 |
| | N8 | |
| | | (398) |
| | 64  JOHANNESBURG | |
| | N1 | |
| 419 | BLOEMFONTEIN | 157 |
| | N1 | |
| | CAPE TOWN  177 | |
| | (1004) | |
| | N8  Klerksdorp | |
| | N12  (308) | |
| | KIMBERLEY | |
| 242 | | 334 |
| | N12  32 | |
| Britstown (253) | | |
| 210 | Barkly West | 366 |
| | 113 | |
| | R31 | |
| Postmasburg (49)  R385 | Campbell  R385 (57) | |
| 97 | | 479 |
| | 97 | |
| | R31 | |
| 0 km | KURUMAN | 576 km |

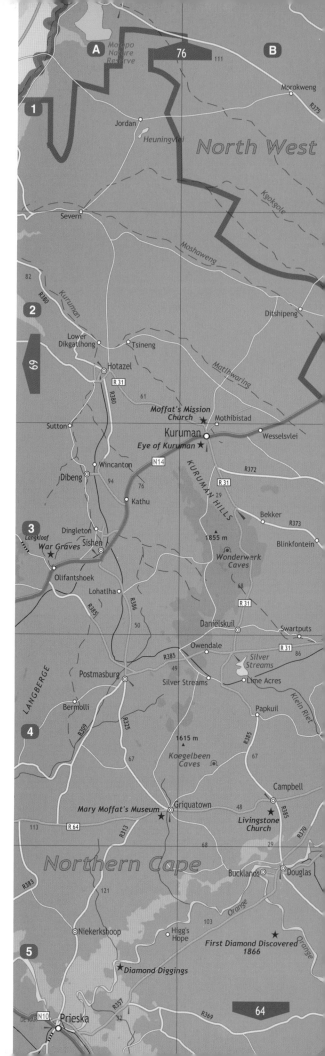

# Northeastern Free State

*T*hough much of the Free State consists of flat, treeless grassland plain, the eastern and southern parts are scenically enchanting, rising in a series of picturesquely weathered sandstone hills, and culminating in the high Maluti Mountains of Lesotho in the east. The countryside is at its most spectacular, perhaps, in the Golden Gate Highlands National Park. This is a fertile region, kind to the growers of maize and wheat, sunflowers, fruit (notably cherries) and vegetables. To the north, around Welkom, there are rich deposits of gold.

## MAIN ATTRACTIONS

**Golden Gate Highlands National Park:** south of Bethlehem; sandstone ridges sculpted by the elements; see antelope and over 160 bird species.
**Vaal River:** border between the Free State and Gauteng; good boating and fishing, especially on the Vaal Dam.

**Africa's Best:** good game-viewing, including white rhino and buffalo, near Ventersburg; tel: (057) 652-2200.
**Pretoriuskloof Bird Sanctuary:** near Bethlehem; tel: (058) 303-2211.
**Bushman paintings:** in the Phutha-ditjhaba area, close to Lesotho.

**Below:** *Travellers are often greeted by large fields of glorious golden yellow sunflowers along the Free State roads. These constitute a major crop in the region which has rich soil, despite relatively poor rainfall and very little surface water.*

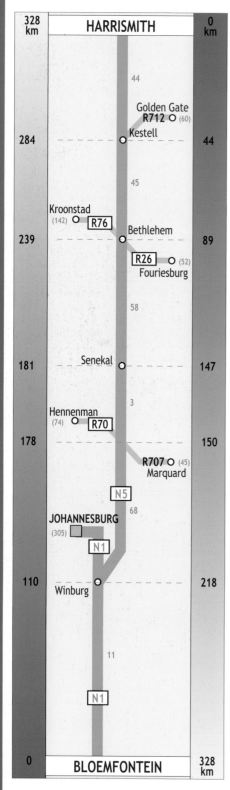

# Northern KwaZulu-Natal

*T*he midlands and northern parts of KwaZulu-Natal, overlooked by the Drakensberg massif to the west, are noted for their rolling green hills, rich farmlands, charming country towns — and for their place in the military annals. For much of the 1800s this region served as an immense battleground as three nations fought bitterly for mastery of the land. Closer to the coast lie the splendours of the iSimangaliso Wetland Park (St Lucia) and some of Africa's very finest wildlife reserves. The seaboard is popular among fisherman and boating enthusiasts; offshore lie the world's southernmost coral reefs, a magnet for scuba divers.

| | | |
|---|---|---|
| 324 km | **EMPANGENI** | 0 km |
| | 46 | |
| | R34 | |
| | Gingindlovu (51) | |
| | R66 | |
| 278 | Nkwalini | 46 |
| | R66 | |
| | 27 | |
| | uLundi (53) | |
| | R66 | |
| 251 | Melmoth | 73 |
| | 93 | |
| | R68 | |
| 158 | Silutshana | 166 |
| | 72 | |
| | Vryheid (67) | |
| | R33 | |
| 86 | | 238 |
| | 2 | |
| 84 | Dundee | 240 |
| | 26 | |
| | R68 | |
| | Newcastle (42) | |
| 58 | | 266 |
| | 58 | |
| | N11 | |
| 0 km | **LADYSMITH** | 324 km |

**Above:** *The Itala Game Reserve, a 30,000ha (74,000-acre) wildlife sanctuary located along the lush banks of the Pongola River, is a haven for the white, or square-lipped, rhino, a highly endangered species. The term 'white' derives from the Afrikaans word 'wyd' (wide) describing the broad, squarish mouth of this mammal.*

## MAIN ATTRACTIONS

**Howick Falls:** outside of Howick, the Mgeni River plunges some 100m (328ft) into a rock pool.

**Hluhluwe and iMfolozi Game Reserves:** the oldest of South Africa's wildlife sanctuaries, these parks sustain a great number of animals and some 400 species of bird. Tel: (035) 562-0848 / 550-8476.

**Itala Game Reserve:** home to some 70 species of mammal, among them both white and black rhino, zebra, giraffe, elephant, brown hyena and various antelope. Beautiful Ntshondwe rest camp is just one accommodation alternative that is available here. Tel: (034) 983-2540.

**Phinda Resource Reserve:** an up-market ecotourist venture that shares its resources with the local communities, while providing the visitor with an exhilarating wilderness experience. Tel: (035) 562-0271.

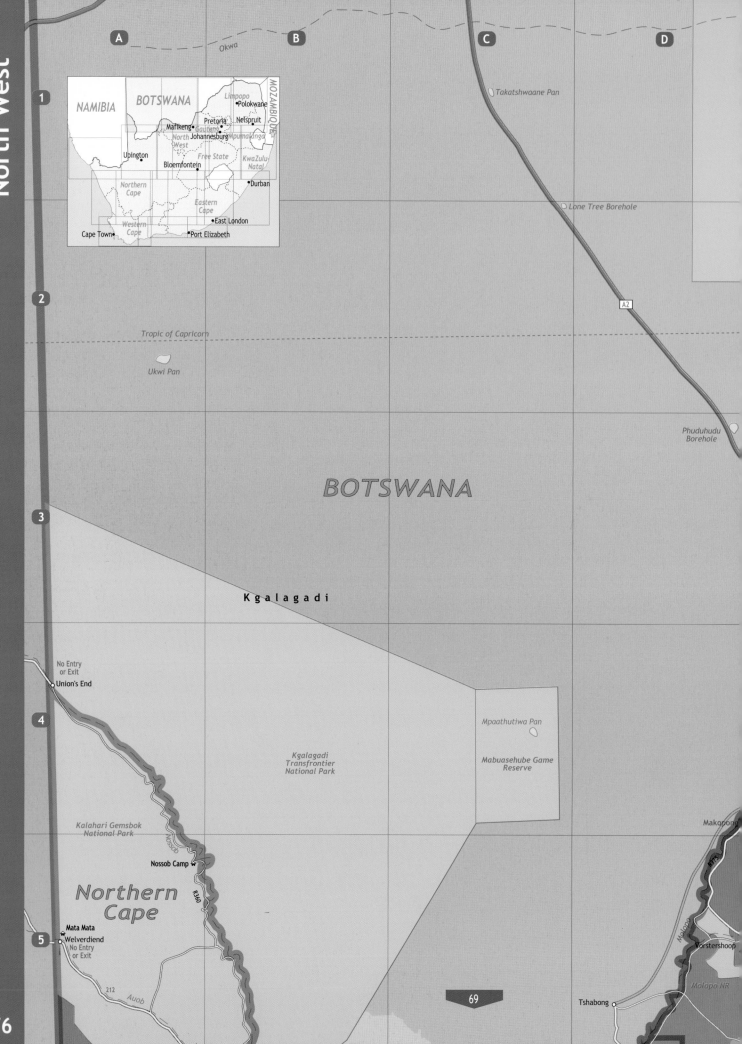

E   F   G   H

1

# BOTSWANA

Central Kalahari Game Reserve

2

Lephepe ○

Sojwe ○

Khutse Game Reserve

Salajwe ○

Boritse Pan

79

Letlhakeng ○

3

A1

Sekoma ○

A2   Jwaneng ○

Molepolole ◉   Mochudi ◉

Khakhea ○

Thamaga ◉   GABORONE

Mosopo ◉

Ramotswa ◉   Madikwe GR

Swartkopfontein

4

Kanye ◉

Lobatse ◉   Skilpadshek

Werda ○   Blairbeth

R375   Livingstone   Pienaar HP
162   Mission

Bray   56   N4

Bray

Terra Firma   R378   Botsalano GR   Zeerust ◉

R375   Ramatlabama ◉   Bewley

Boshoek   64   Moloporivier ○   Molopo   Ramatlabama   68

Senlac ○   Vergelee ○   R52

R375   Labera ○   Mmabatho   Slurry   R505

120   R377   Makgobistad   Mafikeng ◉   83

Tosca ○   Gemsbokvlakte ○   Logageng ○   Rooigrond   Elandsputte

111   128   130   71   N18   63   Bakerville

*North West*

5

77

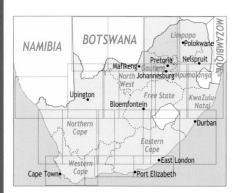

# North West and Limpopo

*T*he North West province is a vast, hot, flattish region of bushveld and thorn, of lonely farmsteads, of fields of sunflowers, groundnuts, tobacco, and citrus, and of villages that sleep soundly in the sun. This is one of the great granaries of southern Africa, with endless fields of maize stretching out to the far horizon. Limpopo, which stretches up the lovely Waterberg and Soutpansberg ranges to the Limpopo River valley, is also largely farming country but more densely populated; its principal centre and capital is the pleasant town of Polokwane.

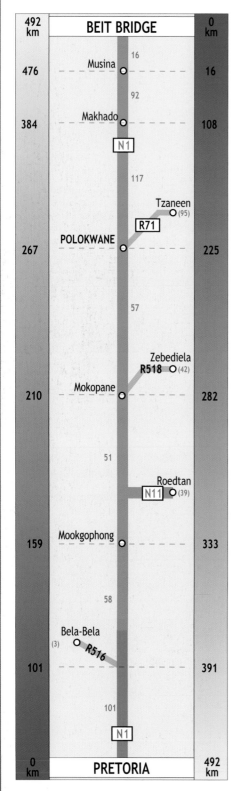

## TRAVEL TIPS

All national roads in this area are tarred and generally in excellent condition; most of the secondary roads are gravelled and reasonably well maintained.

The stretch of road between Bela-Bela and Polokwane can get very busy over the Easter weekend. Holiday-makers travelling to the towns and game reserves of the Lowveld join a cavalcade of taxis and buses ferrying worshippers of the ZCC (Zion Christian Church) to their destination, Moria, near Polokwane. Traffic is congested and extreme caution is advised.

## MAIN ATTRACTIONS

**Sun City and Palace of the Lost City:** luxury hotel-casino complex of pure innovation and fantasy.
**Pilanesberg Game Reserve:** great expanse of wildlife-rich habitat.
**Bela-Bela:** renowned for its curative springs; the Hydro Spa is of world standard.
**Polokwane:** principal town of Limpopo; nearby are the **Percy Fyfe Nature Reserve**, where several antelope species may be seen, and the interesting **Bakone Malapa Open-air Museum**, with traditional *kraal* and handicrafts.

**Below:** *The natural springs at Bela-Bela are not the only attraction at this world-class spa resort.*

A  B  [A1]  C  D

Northern Tuli Conservation Area

Reptile Footprints ★

Serowe

1

Palapye

Zanzibar
Platjan
Kopspruit  Usutu  Gregory
125  R572
Maasstroom  Tonash  De Gracht

Sherwood Ranch

B O T S W A N A

Mahalapye

Martin's Drift
Groblers Bridge
Tom Burke
Swartwater

Blouberg NR

Tolwe

BLOUBERG

Beauty
Marnitz
Baltimore  Woudkop
Glen Alpine Dam

2

Makwate
75
N11

Parr's Halt
Monte Christo
Senwabarana

Tropic of Capricorn
Stockpoort
R572  R510
Oranjefontein
Steilloopbrug

Ons Hoop
Limpopo
Janseput
Marken
178  N11

Lephalale
R518
Villa Nora
160

Mokolo
77

56  Afguns
Lapalala Wilderness GR
Groesbeek  Limburg  Matlala

Mosomane
Spanwerk

Elmeston
Mokolo Dam
Mokolo Dam NR

Mokamole
R518
Tinmyne

3

Rooibokkraal
Rooibosbult
R510
Hermanusdorings
R517

Mahwelereng
Mokopane

Matlabas
41
Moorddrif Monument

Mochudi

Sentrum
66  Manakele NP
Vaalwater
Palala
Doorndraai Dam NR

Maricosdraai
2085 m
W A T E R B E R G E
Klein-Sand
Vanalphensvlei
Haakdoring
N1
N11

Sikwane
Kopfontein Gate
Derdepoort
Oostermoed
Rankin's
Alma  48
Mineral Springs
82  Mookgophong
R520  R519
Roedtan
81

Dwaalboom
WITFONTEINRANT 1499 m
Middelwit
R511
Rooiberg
R516
Modimolle
Middelfontein
75
Crecy
R519

Zwingli
Madikwe GR
Kaya se Put
Ganskuil
105
Koedoeskop
Leeuport
Mabula
Hot Mineral Springs
Holme Park
104
R516

Nietverdiend
Molatedi Dam
Silkaatskop
Northam
R511
Moretele
Bela-Bela
Settlers
R516
Tuinplaas
Nutfield
R33

R49

North West
Assen
Borakalalo Game Reserve
Klipvoor Dam
Radium  54
Rust de Winter

Mabeskraal
PILANESBERG 1687 m
Vaalkop Dam
Atlanta
125
Pienaarsrivier
N1
Styabuswa
R573

Straatsdrif
Mabaalstad
Mogwase
Beestekraal
Rooikoppies Dam
Temba
Babelegi
Dennilton
Witnek

Skuinsdrif
Kromellenboog Dam
Sun City/Lost City
Soutpan
Hammanskraal
Mpumalanga
156
Kwamhlanga

Marico Bosveld NR
Pilanesberg Game Reserve
Mabopane
Tswaing Crater and Museum
Verena
R25

Zeerust
Paul Kruger's Cottage
Bospoort Dam
R556
Pansdrif
Ga-Rankuwa
Seringkop
Cullinan
R544

Groot Marico
Rusverby
Millvale
Syringa Tree Stump
Marikana
Brits
R513
PRETORIA
Rayton
Vaalplaas

Wondermere
N4
Swartruggens  88
Rustenburg
89
Kosmos
Hartbeespoort
N4
11
R513
Bronkhorstspruit
Kromdraai

Carlsonia
Mabaalstad
Koster
Derby
R509
MAGALIESBERG
Magaliesberg Nature Area
Skeerpoort
Erasmia
Centurion
N4
R25
eMalahleni (Witbank)
Balmoral

131
Grootpan
Gauteng
73

81
5
R33

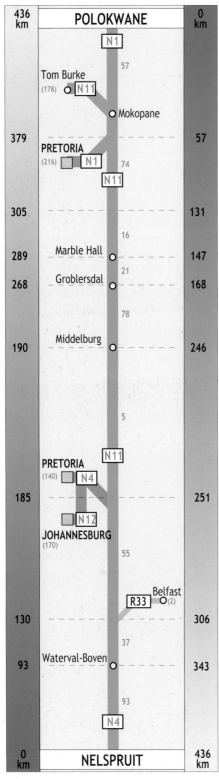

| 436 km | POLOKWANE | 0 km |
|---|---|---|
| | N1 | |
| | 57 | |
| Tom Burke (178) | N11 | |
| | Mokopane | |
| 379 | PRETORIA (216) N1 | 57 |
| | 74 | |
| | N11 | |
| 305 | | 131 |
| | 16 | |
| 289 | Marble Hall | 147 |
| | 21 | |
| 268 | Groblersdal | 168 |
| | 78 | |
| 190 | Middelburg | 246 |
| | 5 | |
| | N11 | |
| | PRETORIA (140) N4 | |
| 185 | | 251 |
| | N12 | |
| | JOHANNESBURG (170) | |
| | 55 | |
| | Belfast (2) R33 | |
| 130 | | 306 |
| | 37 | |
| 93 | Waterval-Boven | 343 |
| | 93 | |
| | N4 | |
| 0 km | NELSPRUIT | 436 km |

# Limpopo and Mpumalanga

*T*he eastern part of this region is dominated by the Great Escarpment, a spectacular compound of forest-mantled mountains, deep ravines, crystal-clear streams and delicate waterfalls. For sheer scenic beauty, few other parts of the country can compare with this imposing range, which rises near Nelspruit and runs to the northeast for some 300km (186 miles). To the east of the escarpment lies the wildlife-rich Lowveld, where the vast Kruger National Park and a host of beautiful private reserves are situated.

## MAIN ATTRACTIONS

**Pilgrim's Rest:** a living showcase of the early gold-mining days.
**Zebediela:** South Africa's largest citrus estates are located here.
**Polokwane:** this is the principal town of Limpopo.
**Tzaneen:** little town surrounded by waterfalls and forests. Visit nearby **Magoebaskloof** and see the **Modjadjiskloof** realm of the **Modjadji Rain Queen** (source for Sir Rider Haggard's novel *She*) and the impressive cycad forest.
**Loskop Dam Game Reserve:** wildlife sanctuary around a large dam.
**The Sunland Baobab:** A 6000-year-old boabab tree near Modjadjiskloof; tel: (015) 309-9039.

## TRAVEL TIPS

Most of the roads are tarred, generally in excellent condition and well sign-posted. The climate is equable, though rainfall during the summer months, from November to February, often occurs in the form of sudden torrential down-pours which are accompanied by thunder and lightning. The storms tend to be brief, however, and there are very few days without long hours of sunshine.
A common feature of the escarpment is the occurrence of dense fog patches, and caution is therefore advised.
During the 19th and early 20th centuries malaria claimed the lives of many settlers in this area.
The disease is largely under control today, but travellers are strongly advised to take precautionary mea-sures before entering the region.

**Below:** *The Blyde River winds its way through the magnificent canyon of the same name.*

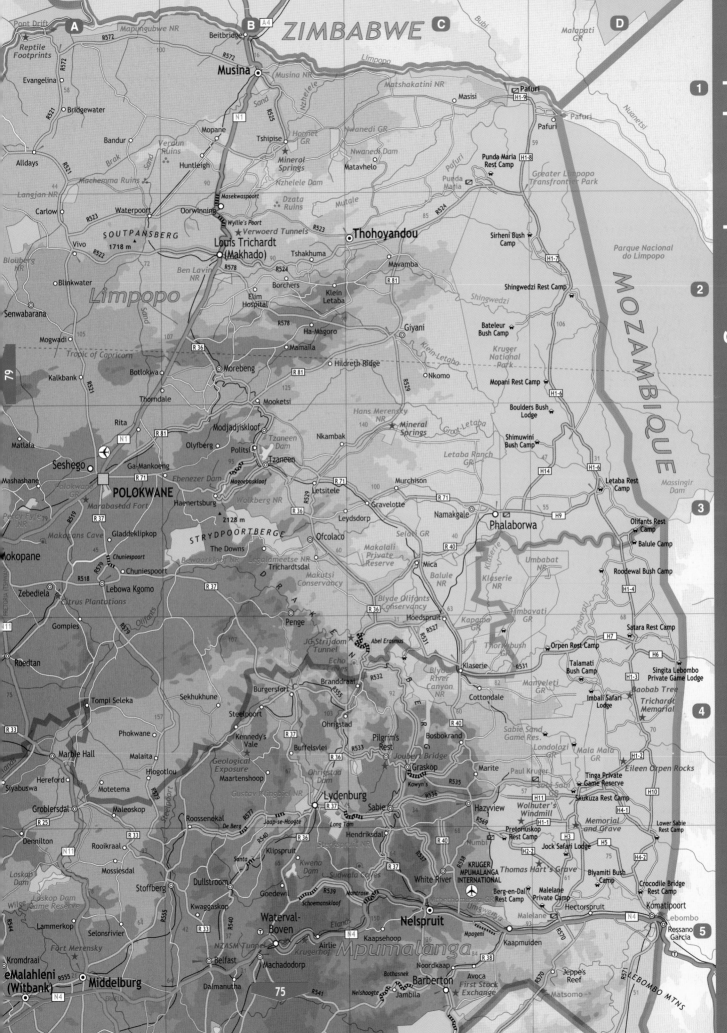

ZIMBABWE

MOZAMBIQUE

Limpopo

Mpumalanga

KRUGER NATIONAL PARK

**Places and features shown on the map:**

Pont Drift, Reptile Footprints, Evangelina, Bridgewater, Bandur, Alldays, Carlow, Vivo, Blouberg NR, Blinkwater, Senwabarana, Mogwadi, Kalkbank, Matlala, Mashashane, Seshego, Polokwane GR, POLOKWANE, Marabastad Fort, Percy Fyfe NR, Makapans Cave, Gladdeklipkop, Mokopane, Zebediela, Citrus Plantations, Gompies, Roedtan, Tompi Seleka, Marble Hall, Hereford, Siyabuswa, Motetema, Groblersdal, Maleoskop, Dennilton, Rooikraal, Mossiesdal, Loskop Dam, Loskop Dam Game Reserve, Lammerkop, Selonsrivier, Fort Merensky, Kromdraai, eMalahleni (Witbank), Middelburg, Belfast, Dalmanutha, Machadodorp

Beitbridge, Musina, Mapungubwe NR, Musina NR, Mopane, Huntleigh, Tshipise, Hornet GR, Verdun Ruins, Mineral Springs, Machemma Ruins, Langjan NR, Waterpoort, Oorwinning, Masekwaspoort, Wyllie's Poort, Verwoerd Tunnels, Dzata Ruins, SOUTPANSBERG, 1718 m, Louis Trichardt (Makhado), Ben Lavin NR, Tshakhuma, Borchers, Elim Hospital, Klein Letaba, Ha-Mágoro, Mamaila, Morebeng, Botlokwa, Thorndale, Mooketsi, Rita, Modjadjiskloof, Olyfberg, Politsi, Tzaneen Dam, Tzaneen, Ebenezer Dam, Ga-Mankoeng, Haenertsberg, Magoebaskloof, Wolkberg NR, 2128 m, Letsitele, Nkambak, The Downs, Bewaarkloof NR, Legalameetse NR, Trichardtsdal, Ofcolaco, STRYDPOORTBERGE, Chuniespoort, Lebowa Kgomo, DRAKENSBERG, Penge, Burgersfort, Sekhukhune, Steelport, Ohrigstad, Kennedy's Vale, Buffelsvlei, Branddraai, JG Strijdom Tunnel, Echo Caves, Abel Erasmus, Phokwane, Malaita, Hlogotlou, Geological Exposure, Maartenshoop, Gustav Klingbiel NR, Ohrigstad Dam, Lydenburg, Pilgrim's Rest, Joubert Bridge, Graskop, Kowyn's, De Berg, Jaap-se-Hoogte, Long Tom, Roossenekal, Klipspruit, Santa, Kwena Dam, Goedewil, Sudwala Caves, Montrose, Schoemanskloof, Dullstroom, Kwaggaskop, Stoffberg, Waterval-Boven, NZASM Tunnel, Krugerhof, Airlie, Kaapschehoop, Machadodorp

Malapati GR, Pafuri, Masisi, Punda Maria Rest Camp, Greater Limpopo Transfrontier Park, Parque Nacional do Limpopo, Sirheni Bush Camp, Mavamba, Giyani, Shingwedzi Rest Camp, Shingwedzi, Bateleur Bush Camp, Kruger National Park, Klein-Letaba, Nkomo, Hildreth Ridge, Mopani Rest Camp, Boulders Bush Lodge, Hans Merensky NR, Mineral Springs, Groot-Letaba, Letaba Ranch GR, Shimuwini Bush Camp, Massingir Dam, Letaba Rest Camp, Olifants Rest Camp, Balule Camp, Roodewal Bush Camp, Murchison, Gravelotte, Leydsdorp, Selati GR, Namakgale, Phalaborwa, Mica, Makalali Private Reserve, Makutsi Conservancy, Balule NR, Umbabat NR, Klaserie NR, Satara Rest Camp, Orpen Rest Camp, Singita Lebombo Private Game Lodge, Timbavati GR, Kapama GR, Thornybush GR, Talamati Bush Camp, Imbali Safari Lodge, Baobab Tree, Trichardt Memorial, Blyde Olifants Conservancy, Hoedspruit, Manyeleti GR, Blyde River Canyon NR, Klaserie, Cottondale, Sabie Sand Game Res, Londolozi, Mala Mala GR, Eileen Orpen Rocks, Bosbokrand, Marite, Paul Kruger, Tinga Private Game Reserve, Skukuza Rest Camp, Sabi Sabi, Hazyview, Wolhuter's Windmill, Memorial and Grave, Pretoriuskop Rest Camp, Numbi, Jock Safari Lodge, Lower Sabie Rest Camp, White River, KRUGER MPUMALANGA INTERNATIONAL, Berg-en-Dal Rest Camp, Thomas Hart's Grave, Malelane Private Camp, Biyamiti Bush Camp, Crocodile Bridge Rest Camp, Malelane, Hectorspruit, Komatipoort, Ressano Garcia, Nelspruit, Kaapmuiden, LEBOMBO MTNS, Noordkaap, Avoca, First Stock Exchange, Bothasnek, Jambila, Barberton, Nelshoogte, Jeppe's Reef, Matsomo

**Road numbers:** R572, A4, R525, N1, R521, R523, R522, R578, R524, R81, R36, R71, N11, R37, R519, R518, R579, R532, R555, R533, R535, R536, R540, R541, R544, R577, R570, R571, R538, R569, R537, R40, R531, R527, R25, R33, N4, R35, R521, R529, R578

**Grid references:** H1-9, H1-8, H1-7, H1-6, H14, H9, H1-4, H7, H6, H1-3, H1-2, H10, H4-1, H11, H1-1, H3, H5, H2-2, H4-2

79

75

# TOURIST AREA AND TEXT INDEX

Note: Numbers in **bold** denote photographs

| | | | | | | | |
|---|---|---|---|---|---|---|---|
| Coffee Bay | 33 | Durban | **28** | Fort Mtombeni | 32 | Haga-Haga | 33 |
| Cofimvaba | 33 | Golden Mile | **67** | Fouriesburg | 55 | Halcyon Drift | 33 |
| Coghlan | 33 | Durbanville | 40 | Frankfort | 35 | Hamburg | 35 |
| Colchester | 34 | Dwarskersbos | 45 | | 55 | Hankey | 34 |
| Coldstream | 39 | Dwarsrand | 25 | Franklin | 33 | Hantam | 45 |
| Colenso | 31 | Dysselsdorp | 38 | Frasers Camp | 35 | Harding | 33 |
| | 32 | | | FREE STATE | **54** | Harper | 35 |
| | 55 | **E**ast London | 35 | | **72** | Harrisburg | 55 |
| Committees | 35 | Eastpoort | 34 | Frere | 32 | Harrismith | 31 |
| Commondale | 32 | Edenburg | 55 | | | | 55 |
| Constantia | 46 | Edendale | 27 | **G**andhi Settlement | 28 | Hartbeespoort Dam | 10 |
| Content | 55 | | 31 | Garies | 45 | Hartenbos | 38 |
| Cookhouse | 34 | Edenville | 55 | Garryowen | 33 | Hattingspruit | 32 |
| Coombs | 35 | Edinglassie | 27 | Geluksberg | 31 | Hazyview | 21 |
| Cornelia | 55 | Eendekuil | 45 | Gemvale | 33 | | 22 |
| Cottondale | 21 | Ekuseni | 25 | Geneva | 55 | Hectorspruit | 21 |
| | 22 | Ekutuleni | 25 | George | 38 | | 22 |
| Cradock | 64 | Elandsbaai | 45 | | 40 | Heerenlogement | 45 |
| Craigsforth | 31 | | 45 | Gingindlovu | 25 | Heidelberg | 55 |
| Crossroads | 35 | Elandshoek | 21 | | 32 | Heilbron | 55 |
| Curry's Post | 31 | Elandskraal | 32 | Gladstone | 35 | Helpmekaar | 32 |
| | | Elandslaagte | 32 | Glen Beulah | 27 | Hemlock | 22 |
| **D**almanutha | 22 | elephant | **20** | Glen Echo | 27 | Hendriksdal | 21 |
| Dalton | 32 | Elliot | 33 | Glenashley | 27 | | 22 |
| Damwal | 22 | Elliotdale | 33 | Glencoe | 32 | Hennenman | 55 |
| Danielsrus | 55 | embassies | | | 55 | Hereford | 22 |
| Dannhauser | 32 | (international) | 16 | Glenconnor | 34 | Hermanus | 59 |
| Dargle | 31 | Embotyi | 33 | Glenmore Beach | 27 | Herold | 38 |
| Darling | 45 | Empangeni | 25 | | 33 | Heroldsbaai | 38 |
| Darnall | 25 | | 32 | Glenrock | 55 | Herschel | 55 |
| | 32 | Enon | 34 | Glentana | 38 | Hertzogville | 55 |
| Daskop | 38 | Entumeni | 25 | Gluckstadt | 32 | Het Kruis | 45 |
| De Brug | 55 | | 32 | God's Window | 22 | Heuningspruit | 55 |
| De Hoek | 45 | eNyamazaneni | 22 | Goedemoed | 55 | Hex River Valley | **42** |
| De Vlug | 39 | Escombe | 27 | Goedewil | 22 | Hibberdene | 27 |
| Dealesville | 55 | Eshowe | 25 | Gold Reef City | 12 | Hibberds | 25 |
| Deepdale | 31 | | 32 | Golden Valley | 34 | high commissions | |
| Delportshoop | 55 | Esikhawini | 25 | Gompies | 22 | (international) | 16 |
| Demistkraal | 34 | Esperanza | 27 | Gonubie | 35 | Highflats | 27 |
| Deneysville | 55 | Estcourt | 31 | Gonzana | 35 | Highveld | 10 |
| Dennitlon | 22 | | 32 | Gqweta | 21 | Hillcrest | 27 |
| Despatch | 34 | | 55 | Graaff-Reinet | 64 | Himeville | 31 |
| Dewetsdorp | 55 | Eston | 27 | Graafwater | 45 | Hlabisa | 25 |
| Die Hoek | 39 | Evaton | 55 | Grahamstown | **35** | | 32 |
| Dimbaza | 35 | Excelsior | 55 | | 35 | Hlobane | 32 |
| Diphuti | 21 | | | GrandWest Casino | 46 | Hlogotlou | 22 |
| Dlolwana | 32 | **F**allodon | 35 | Graskop | | Hlomela | 21 |
| Dlomodlomo | 25 | Fauresmith | 55 | | 22 | Hlotse | 55 |
| Donkerpoort | 55 | Felixton | 25 | Graspan | 55 | Hluhluwe | 25 |
| Dordrecht | 55 | | 32 | Greenmarket Square | 49 | | 32 |
| Doringbaai | 45 | Ferreira | 55 | Greystone | 34 | Hlutankungu | 27 |
| Doringbos | 45 | Ficksburg | 55 | Greytown | 32 | Hobeni | 33 |
| Douglas | 55 | Fitzsimon's | | Groblersdal | 22 | Hobhouse | 55 |
| Dover | 55 | Snake Park | 28 | Groenriviersmond | 45 | Hoedspruit | 21 |
| Drakensberg | **30** | Flagstaff | 33 | Groenvlei | 32 | Hoekwil | 38 |
| Driefontein | 32 | Florisbad | 55 | Groot-Brakrivier | 38 | Hogsback | 35 |
| Dublin | 21 | Forestry Station | 34 | Grootdrif | 45 | | 35 |
| Dududu | 27 | Fort Beaufort | 35 | Grootspruit | 32 | Hole-in-the-Wall | 33 |
| Dullstroom | 22 | Fort Brown | 35 | Grootvlei | 55 | Holy Cross | 33 |
| Dundee | 32 | Fort Donald | 33 | Gumtree | 55 | Hoopstad | 55 |
| | 55 | Fort Frederick | 36 | | | Hopefield | 45 |
| Dupelston | 55 | Fort Hare | 35 | **H**aarlem | 39 | Hopewell | 34 |

| Place | Page |
|---|---|
| Pongola | 32 |
| Pools | 45 |
| Port Alfred | 35 |
| Port Edward | 27 |
| | 33 |
| Port Elizabeth | 34 |
| Port Grosvenor | 33 |
| Port Shepstone | 27 |
| | 33 |
| Port St Johns | 33 |
| Porterville | 45 |
| Portobello Beach | 27 |
| Potchefstroom | 55 |
| Potsdam | 35 |
| Prince Alfred Hamlet | 45 |
| Pretoria | **16** |
| Pretoriuskloof Bird Park | 72 |
| Priors | 55 |
| Prudhou | 35 |
| Punzana | 35 |
| Qamata | 33 |
| Qiba | 33 |
| Qholhora Mouth | 33 |
| Qhora Mouth | 33 |
| Qoboqobo | 33 |
| Qudeni | 32 |
| Queensburgh | 27 |
| Quko | 33 |
| Qumbu | 33 |
| Raisethorpe | 31 |
| Ramsgate | 27 |
| | 33 |
| Randalhurst | 32 |
| Ratanga Junction | 46 |
| Ratelfontein | 45 |
| Rawsonville | 45 |
| Redcliffe | 31 |
| | 32 |
| Reddersdorp | 55 |
| Redelinghuys | 45 |
| Redoubt | 33 |
| Reebokrand | 55 |
| Reitz | 55 |
| Reitzburg | 55 |
| Renosterspruit | 55 |
| Ressano Garcia | 21 |
| rhino (white) | **74** |
| Rhodes Memorial | 49 |
| Richards Bay | 25 |
| | 32 |
| Richmond | 27 |
| Riebeeckstad | 55 |
| Riebeek Kasteel | 45 |
| Riebeek-Oos | 35 |
| Riebeek-Wes | 45 |
| Rietkuil | 55 |
| Rietpoort | 45 |
| Rietvlei | 31 |
| Rietvlei | 32 |
| Ritchie | 55 |
| River View | 25 |
| | 32 |
| Robben Island | 47 |
| | 53 |
| Rockmount | 31 |
| Rode | 33 |
| Roedtan | 22 |
| Roma | 55 |
| Rooikraal | 22 |
| Rooipan | 55 |
| Rooiwal | 55 |
| Roosboom | 31 |
| | 32 |
| Roossenekal | 22 |
| Rorke's Drift | 32 |
| Rosebank | 27 |
| Rosemoor | 38 |
| Rosendal | 55 |
| Rosetta | 31 |
| | 32 |
| Rossouw | 55 |
| Rouxville | 55 |
| Rust | 45 |
| Rustig | 55 |
| Saasveld | 38 |
| Sabie | 21 |
| | 22 |
| Saldanha | 45 |
| Salem | 35 |
| Salt Lake | 55 |
| Sand River Valley | 31 |
| Sandberg | 45 |
| Sandton | 12 |
| Sannaspos | 55 |
| Sasolburg | 55 |
| Sauer | 45 |
| Sawoti | 27 |
| Schmidtsdrif | 55 |
| Scottburgh | **26** |
| | 27 |
| Sea Park | 27 |
| Sea View | 34 |
| Sebapala | 55 |
| Sedgefield | 38 |
| Sefako | 55 |
| Sekhukhune | 22 |
| Selonsrivier | 22 |
| Senekal | 55 |
| Seven Fountains | 35 |
| Sevenoaks | 32 |
| Sezela | 27 |
| Shakaland | 24 |
| Shallcross | 27 |
| Shannon | 55 |
| Sheldon | 34 |
| Sidbury | 35 |
| Sidwadweni | 33 |
| Signal Hill | 49 |
| Sihlengeni | 25 |
| Silutshana | 32 |
| Simon's Town | 46 |
| Sinksabrug | 38 |
| Sittingbourne | 35 |
| Siyabuswa | 22 |
| Skoenmakerskop | 34 |
| Smithfield | 55 |
| Sneezewood | 33 |
| Sodwana Bay | 24 |
| Somerset East | 34 |
| Somkele | 25 |
| | 32 |
| South Downs | 31 |
| Southbroom | 27 |
| | 33 |
| Southeyville | 33 |
| Southwell | 35 |
| Soutpan | 55 |
| Soweto | 10 |
| | 12 |
| | 55 |
| Spes Bona | 55 |
| Springfontein | 55 |
| Spytfontein | 55 |
| St Faith's | 27 |
| St Francis Bay | 34 |
| St Helena Bay | 45 |
| St Lucia | **24** |
| | 25 |
| St Matthew's | 35 |
| St Michaels on Sea | 27 |
| Stafford's Post | 33 |
| Stanger | 32 |
| Steelpoort | 21 |
| | 22 |
| Steilrand | 32 |
| Stellenbosch | 42 |
| | 44 |
| Sterkspruit | 55 |
| Sterkstroom | 55 |
| Steynsburg | 55 |
| Steynsrus | 55 |
| Stilfontein | 55 |
| Stoffberg | 22 |
| Stompneusbaai | 45 |
| Stoneyridge | 33 |
| Stormberg | 55 |
| Stormsrivier | 39 |
| Strandfontein | 45 |
| Summerstrand | 34 |
| Sun City — Palace of the Lost City | **18** |
| Sundumbili | 25 |
| Sunland | 34 |
| Swart Umfolozi | 32 |
| Swartkops | 34 |
| Swempoort | 55 |
| Swinburne | 55 |
| Syfergat | 55 |
| Tabankulu | 33 |
| Table Mountain | **49** |
| Table Mounatin | **52** |
| Tainton | 35 |
| Taleni | 33 |
| Tanga | 35 |
| Tatafalaza | 25 |
| Tergniet | 38 |
| Teyateyaneng | 55 |
| Teza | 32 |
| Thaba 'Nchu | 55 |
| The Berg | 22 |
| The Crags | 39 |
| The Downs | 21 |
| The Grove | 31 |
| The Haven | 33 |
| The Heads | 39 |
| The Ranch | 32 |
| Theron | 55 |
| Theunissen | 55 |
| Tidbury's Toll | 35 |
| Tierfontein | 55 |
| Tierpoort | 55 |
| Tina Bridge | 33 |
| Tip Tree | 34 |
| Toggekry | 25 |
| Tombo | 33 |
| Tompi Seleka | 22 |
| Tongaat Beach | 27 |
| Trafalgar | 27 |
| Trawal | 45 |
| Trichardtsdal | 21 |
| Triple Streams | 33 |
| Trompsburg | 55 |
| Tshani | 33 |
| Tsitsa Bridge | 33 |
| Tsitsikamma Trail | **39** |
| Tsolo | 33 |
| Tsomo | 33 |
| Tugela Ferry | 32 |
| Tugela Mouth | 25 |
| | 32 |
| Tulbagh | 45 |
| Tweeling | 55 |
| Tweeriviere | 39 |
| Tweespruit | 55 |
| Two Oceans Aquarium | 52 |
| Tyata | 35 |
| Tyira | 33 |
| Tzaneen | 80 |
| Ubombo | 25 |
| | 32 |
| Ugie | 33 |
| Uitenhage | 34 |
| Uitspankraal | 45 |
| uLundi | 25 |
| | 32 |
| uMbogintwini | 27 |
| uMbumbulu | 27 |
| uMdloti | 27 |
| uMgeni Dam | 27 |
| uMhlanga | 27 |
| uMkomaas | 27 |

# MAIN MAP INDEX

| Place | Grid | Pg | Place | Grid | Pg | Place | Grid | Pg | Place | Grid | Pg |
|---|---|---|---|---|---|---|---|---|---|---|---|
| Brits | C5 | 79 | Clanville | B3 | 66 | De Doorns | C1 | 60 | Dwarskersbos | C5 | 62 |
| Britstown | B2 | 64 | Clanwilliam | D4 | 63 | De Gracht | D1 | 79 | Dwyka | G5 | 63 |
| Broedersput | D2 | 71 | Clarens | B4 | 73 | De Hoek | D5 | 63 | Dysselsdorp | A4 | 60 |
| Bronkhorstspruit | C1 | 73 | Clarkebury | C4 | 66 | De Hoop | A4 | 60 | East London | G4 | 61 |
| Brooks Nek | D2 | 66 | Clarkson | C5 | 60 | De Klerk | B3 | 64 | Eastpoort | E5 | 65 |
| Bruintjieshoogte | E5 | 65 | Clewer | C1 | 73 | De Rust | A4 | 60 | Edenburg | E1 | 65 |
| Bucklands | B5 | 70 | Clifford | B3 | 66 | Dealesville | E4 | 71 | Edendale | A1 | 67 |
| Buffelsdrif | B5 | 60 | Clocolan | A4 | 73 | Deelfontein | C3 | 65 | Edenville | B3 | 73 |
| Buffelsvlei | B4 | 81 | Coalville | C1 | 73 | Deelpan | E1 | 71 | Eendekuil | D5 | 63 |
| Bulletrap | B1 | 62 | Coega | E5 | 61 | Delareyville | D2 | 71 | Eksteenfontein | B5 | 68 |
| Bultfontein | E4 | 71 | Coerney | E4 | 61 | Delmas | C1 | 73 | Elands Height | C2 | 66 |
| Bulwer | A1 | 67 | Coffee Bay | D4 | 66 | Delportshoop | C4 | 71 | Elandsbaai | C4 | 62 |
| Buntingville | D4 | 66 | Cofimvaba | B4 | 66 | Demistkraal | D5 | 60 | Elandsdrift | E4 | 65 |
| Burgersdorp | F3 | 65 | Coghlan | C4 | 66 | Deneysville | B2 | 73 | Elandskraal | A4 | 75 |
| Burgersfort | B4 | 81 | Colchester | E5 | 61 | Dennilton | A5 | 81 | Elandslaagte | D4 | 73 |
| Burgervilleweg | C2 | 65 | Colenso | D4 | 73 | Derby | B5 | 79 | Elandsputte | E1 | 71 |
| Butterworth | C4 | 66 | Colesberg | D2 | 65 | Derdepoort | A4 | 79 | Elgin | B2 | 60 |
| Cala | B3 | 66 | Coleskeplaas | C5 | 60 | Despatch | D5 | 60 | Elim | C3 | 60 |
| Cala Road | B3 | 66 | Coligny | E1 | 71 | Devon | C1 | 73 | Elim Hospital | B2 | 81 |
| Caledon | C3 | 60 | Committees | F4 | 61 | Devonlea | D2 | 71 | Elliot | B3 | 66 |
| Calitzdorp | E2 | 61 | Commondale | B3 | 75 | Dewetsdorp | F1 | 65 | Elliotdale | C4 | 66 |
| Calvert | B3 | 75 | Concordia | C5 | 68 | Dibeng | A3 | 70 | Elmeston | C3 | 79 |
| Calvinia | E3 | 63 | Content | D4 | 71 | Die Bos | E4 | 63 | Eloff | C1 | 73 |
| Cambria | C5 | 60 | Conway | E4 | 65 | Die Dam | C3 | 60 | eMalahleni | | |
| Cameron Glen | E4 | 65 | Cookhouse | E5 | 65 | Die Vlug | B5 | 60 | (Witbank) | D1 | 73 |
| Campbell | B4 | 70 | Copperton | A1 | 64 | Diemansputs | G1 | 63 | eMangusi | D2 | 75 |
| Candover | C3 | 75 | Cornelia | C2 | 73 | Dieput | C2 | 65 | eMpangeni | C5 | 75 |
| Cape St Francis | D5 | 60 | Cottondale | C4 | 81 | Dingleton | A3 | 70 | eNtumeni | B5 | 75 |
| Cape Town | B2 | 60 | Cradock | E4 | 65 | Dirkiesdorp | A2 | 75 | Erasmia | B1 | 73 |
| Carletonville | A1 | 73 | Cramond | C2 | 69 | Ditshipeng | B2 | 70 | Ermelo | D2 | 73 |
| Carlisle Bridge | F5 | 65 | Crecy | D4 | 79 | Dlolwana | B4 | 75 | eShowe | B5 | 75 |
| Carlsonia | A5 | 79 | Creighton | A2 | 67 | Dohne | B5 | 66 | Estcourt | D5 | 73 |
| Carlton | D3 | 65 | Cullinan | D5 | 79 | Donkerpoort | E2 | 65 | Evander | C2 | 73 |
| Carnarvon | A3 | 64 | Dabenoris | D5 | 68 | Donnybrook | A2 | 67 | Evangelina | A1 | 81 |
| Carolina | A1 | 75 | Dagbreek | C4 | 69 | Dordrecht | B3 | 66 | Evaton | B2 | 73 |
| Cathcart | B4 | 66 | Daggaboersnek | E5 | 65 | Doringbaai | C4 | 62 | Excelsior | F5 | 71 |
| Cedarville | D2 | 66 | Daleside | B1 | 73 | Doringbos | D4 | 63 | Fairfield | C3 | 60 |
| Cederberg | D5 | 63 | Dalmanutha | A1 | 75 | Douglas | B5 | 70 | Faure | B2 | 60 |
| Centani | C5 | 66 | Dalton | B1 | 67 | Dover | B2 | 73 | Fauresmith | E1 | 65 |
| Centurion | B1 | 73 | Daniëlskuil | B3 | 70 | Dovesdale | A1 | 73 | Felixton | C5 | 75 |
| Ceres | C1 | 60 | Danielsrus | B3 | 73 | Drennan | E4 | 65 | Ferreira | E5 | 71 |
| Chalumna | G4 | 61 | Dannhauser | A3 | 75 | Driefontein | D4 | 73 | Ficksburg | B4 | 73 |
| Charl Cilliers | C2 | 73 | Darling | B1 | 60 | Droërivier | A4 | 64 | Firgrove | B2 | 60 |
| Charlestown | D3 | 73 | Darnall | B5 | 75 | Dullstroom | B5 | 81 | Fish Hoek | B2 | 60 |
| Chieveley | D5 | 73 | Daskop | A5 | 60 | Dundee | A4 | 75 | Flagstaff | D3 | 66 |
| Chintsa East | C5 | 66 | Dasville | C2 | 73 | Dupleston | F2 | 65 | Florisbad | E4 | 71 |
| Chrissiesmeer | A1 | 75 | Davel | D2 | 73 | Durban | B2 | 67 | Fochville | A2 | 73 |
| Christiana | D3 | 71 | Daveyton | C1 | 73 | Durbanville | B2 | 60 | Fort Beaufort | F5 | 65 |
| Chuniespoort | A3 | 81 | Dawn | G4 | 61 | Dutywa | C4 | 66 | Fort Brown | F5 | 65 |
| Churchhaven | A1 | 60 | De Aar | C2 | 65 | Dwaal | D3 | 65 | Fort Donald | D3 | 66 |
| Citrusdal | D5 | 63 | De Brug | E5 | 71 | Dwaalboom | A4 | 79 | Fort Hare | F4 | 61 |

| Name | Ref | Pg | Name | Ref | Pg | Name | Ref | Pg | Name | Ref | Pg |
|---|---|---|---|---|---|---|---|---|---|---|---|
| Fort Mistake | D4 | 73 | Granaatboskolk | E1 | 63 | Hartebeeskop | B1 | 75 | Hotagterklip | C3 | 60 |
| Fort Mtombeni | B5 | 75 | Graskop | C4 | 81 | Hartswater | D3 | 71 | Hotazel | A2 | 70 |
| Fouriesburg | B4 | 73 | Grasmere | B1 | 73 | Hattingspruit | A4 | 75 | Hottentotskloof | C1 | 60 |
| Frankfort | D3 | 73 | Graspan | C5 | 71 | Hauptsrus | E2 | 71 | Hout Bay | B2 | 60 |
| Franklin | D2 | 66 | Gravelotte | C3 | 81 | Hawston | C3 | 60 | Houtkraal | C2 | 65 |
| Franschhoek | C2 | 60 | Gregory | D1 | 79 | Hazyview | C4 | 81 | Howick | A5 | 75 |
| Fransenhof | A1 | 64 | Greylingstad | C2 | 73 | Hectorspruit | D5 | 81 | Humansdorp | D5 | 60 |
| Fraserburg | G4 | 63 | Greystone | D4 | 60 | Heerenlogement | C4 | 62 | Huntleigh | B1 | 81 |
| Frere | D5 | 73 | Greyton | C2 | 60 | Heidelberg | B2 | 73 | Hutchinson | B3 | 64 |
| Ga-Mankoeng | B3 | 81 | Greytown | A5 | 75 | Heilbron | B2 | 73 | iMpendle | A1 | 67 |
| Gamoep | C1 | 62 | Griquatown | A4 | 70 | Helpmekaar | A4 | 75 | Impisi | A3 | 67 |
| Gansbaai | C3 | 60 | Groblersdal | A4 | 81 | Helvetia | F1 | 65 | iNanda | B1 | 67 |
| Ganskuil | A4 | 79 | Groblershoop | D4 | 69 | Hendriksdal | C5 | 81 | Indwe | B3 | 66 |
| Ganyesa | C1 | 71 | Groenriviers-mond | B3 | 62 | Hendrina | D1 | 73 | Infanta | D3 | 60 |
| Ga-Rankuwa | C5 | 79 | Groenvlei | A3 | 75 | Hennenman | F3 | 71 | Ingogo | D3 | 73 |
| Garies | B2 | 62 | Groesbeek | D3 | 79 | Herbertsdale | E2 | 61 | iNgwavuma | C3 | 75 |
| Garryowen | B3 | 66 | Grondneus | B3 | 69 | Hereford | A4 | 81 | iSipingo | B2 | 67 |
| Geluksburg | D4 | 73 | Groot-Brakrivier | A5 | 60 | Hermanus | C3 | 60 | Iswepe | A2 | 75 |
| Gelukspruit | B3 | 69 | Grootdrif | D3 | 63 | Hermanusdorings | C3 | 79 | Itsoseng | E1 | 71 |
| Gemsbokvlakte | F5 | 77 | Grootdrink | C4 | 69 | Herold | A5 | 60 | iXopo | A2 | 67 |
| Gemvale | D3 | 66 | Groot Jongensfontein | E3 | 61 | Herolds Bay | A5 | 60 | Jacobsdal | C5 | 71 |
| Genadendal | C2 | 60 | Grootkraal | A4 | 60 | Herschel | B2 | 66 | Jagersfontein | E1 | 65 |
| Geneva | F3 | 71 | Groot-Marico | A5 | 79 | Hertzogville | D3 | 71 | Jaght Drift | F1 | 63 |
| George | A5 | 60 | Grootmis | A1 | 62 | Het Kruis | D5 | 63 | Jambila | C5 | 81 |
| Gerdau | E1 | 71 | Grootpan | A5 | 79 | Heuningspruit | A3 | 73 | Jamestown | F3 | 65 |
| Germiston | B1 | 73 | Grootspruit | A3 | 75 | Heydon | D3 | 65 | Jammerdrif | A1 | 66 |
| Geysdorp | D1 | 71 | Grootvlei | C2 | 73 | Hibberdene | B2 | 67 | Jan Kempdorp | D3 | 71 |
| Giesenskraal | B2 | 64 | Groutville | C1 | 67 | Higg's Hope | A5 | 70 | Jansenville | D4 | 60 |
| Gilead | D3 | 79 | Gumtree | A4 | 73 | Highflats | A2 | 67 | Janseput | C2 | 79 |
| Gingindlovu | B5 | 75 | Haakdoring | D3 | 79 | Hilandale | D1 | 60 | Jeffreys Bay | D5 | 60 |
| Giyani | C2 | 81 | Haarlem | B5 | 60 | Hildreth Ridge | B2 | 81 | Jeppe's Reef | D5 | 81 |
| Gladdeklipkop | A3 | 81 | Haenertsburg | B3 | 81 | Hillandale | F5 | 63 | Joel's Drift | B4 | 73 |
| Glencoe | A4 | 75 | Haga-Haga | C5 | 66 | Hilton | A1 | 67 | Johannesburg | B1 | 73 |
| Glenconnor | D4 | 60 | Halcyon Drift | C3 | 66 | Himeville | D1 | 66 | Joubertina | C5 | 60 |
| Glenmore Beach | A3 | 67 | Halfweg | E2 | 63 | Hlabisa | C4 | 75 | Jozini | C3 | 75 |
| Glenrock | F5 | 71 | Ha-Magoro | B2 | 81 | Hlobane | B3 | 75 | Kaapmuiden | C5 | 81 |
| Gloria | D1 | 73 | Hamburg | G4 | 61 | Hlogotlou | A4 | 81 | Kaapsehoop | C5 | 81 |
| Glückstadt | B4 | 75 | Hammanskraal | C5 | 79 | Hluhluwe | C4 | 75 | Kakamas | B4 | 69 |
| Goedemoed | F2 | 65 | Hammarsdale | B1 | 67 | Hobeni | D4 | 66 | Kalbaskraal | B2 | 60 |
| Goedewil | B5 | 81 | Hankey | D5 | 60 | Hobhouse | F5 | 71 | Kalkbank | A2 | 81 |
| Golela | C3 | 75 | Hanover Road | D3 | 65 | Hoedspruit | C4 | 81 | Kalkwerf | C4 | 69 |
| Gompies | A4 | 81 | Hanover | D3 | 65 | Hofmeyr | E3 | 65 | Kameel | D2 | 71 |
| Gonubie | G4 | 61 | Hantam | D3 | 63 | Hogsback | A5 | 66 | Kamiesberg | C2 | 62 |
| Goodhouse | C5 | 68 | Harding | A2 | 67 | Holbank | A2 | 75 | Kamieskroon | B2 | 62 |
| Gordon's Bay | B2 | 60 | Harrisburg | F2 | 71 | Holme Park | D4 | 79 | Kammiebos | C5 | 60 |
| Gouda | B1 | 60 | Harrisdale | B3 | 69 | Holmedene | C2 | 73 | Kanoneiland | C4 | 69 |
| Gouritsmond | E3 | 61 | Harrismith | C4 | 73 | Hondefontein | G4 | 63 | Karatara | B5 | 60 |
| Graaff-Reinet | D4 | 65 | Hartbeesfontein | F2 | 71 | Hondeklipbaai | A2 | 62 | Karee | E4 | 71 |
| Graafwater | C4 | 62 | Hartbeespoort | C5 | 79 | Hoopstad | E3 | 71 | Kareeboschkolk | E1 | 63 |
| Grabouw | B2 | 60 | | | | Hopefield | B1 | 60 | Kareedouw | C5 | 60 |
| Grahamstown | F4 | 61 | | | | Hopetown | C1 | 65 | Karkams | B2 | 62 |

| | | | | | | | | | | |
|---|---|---|---|---|---|---|---|---|---|---|
| Karos | C4 | 69 | Koffiefontein | D1 | 65 | Ladismith | E1 | 61 | Louisvale | C4 | 69 |
| Kasouga | F5 | 61 | Koingnaas | A2 | 62 | Lady Frere | B4 | 66 | Louterwater | C5 | 60 |
| Katkop | E2 | 63 | Kokstad | D2 | 66 | Lady Grey | B2 | 66 | Louwsburg | B3 | 75 |
| Kathu | A3 | 70 | Komaggas | B1 | 62 | Ladybrand | A5 | 73 | Lower | | |
| Kaya se Put | A4 | 79 | Komatipoort | D5 | 81 | Ladysmith | D4 | 73 | Dikgatlhong | A2 | 70 |
| Keate's Drift | A5 | 75 | Komga | B5 | 66 | L'Agulhas | D3 | 60 | Lower Pitseng | C2 | 66 |
| Kei Mouth | C5 | 66 | Komkans | C3 | 62 | Lahlangubo | C3 | 66 | Loxton | A3 | 64 |
| Kei Road | B5 | 66 | Kommandokraal | B5 | 64 | Laingsburg | D1 | 60 | Luckhoff | D1 | 65 |
| Keimoes | B4 | 69 | Kommetjie | B2 | 60 | Lambert's Bay | C4 | 62 | Lundin's Nek | B2 | 66 |
| Keiskammahoek | B5 | 66 | Kommissiepoort | A5 | 73 | Lammerkop | A5 | 81 | Luneberg | A3 | 75 |
| Kempton Park | B1 | 73 | Koopan Suid | B2 | 69 | Landplaas | C3 | 62 | Lusikisiki | D3 | 66 |
| Kendal | C1 | 73 | Koopmansfontein | C4 | 71 | Langberg | E2 | 61 | Luttig | A5 | 64 |
| Kendrew | D5 | 65 | Koosfontein | D2 | 71 | Langdon | C4 | 66 | Lutzputs | B4 | 69 |
| Kenhardt | C5 | 69 | Kootjieskolk | E3 | 63 | Langebaan | A1 | 60 | Lutzville | C4 | 62 |
| Kenilworth | D4 | 71 | Koperspruit | D1 | 79 | Langholm | F4 | 61 | Lydenburg | B4 | 81 |
| Kennedy's Vale | B4 | 81 | Koppies | A2 | 73 | Langklip | B4 | 69 | Lykso | C2 | 71 |
| Kenton on Sea | F5 | 61 | Koringberg | B1 | 60 | Leandra | C1 | 73 | Maartenshoop | B4 | 81 |
| Kestell | C4 | 73 | Koringplaas | F5 | 63 | Lebowa Kgomo | A3 | 81 | Maasstroom | D1 | 79 |
| Kidd's Beach | G4 | 61 | Kosmos | C5 | 79 | Leeudoringstad | E2 | 71 | Mabaalstad | A5 | 79 |
| Kimberley | C4 | 71 | Koster | B5 | 79 | Leeu-Gamka | G5 | 63 | Mabeskraal | A4 | 79 |
| King William's | | | Kotzesrus | B3 | 62 | Leeuport | C4 | 79 | Mabopane | C5 | 79 |
| Town | B5 | 66 | Koukraal | F2 | 65 | Lehlohonolo | D2 | 66 | Mabula | C4 | 79 |
| Kingsburgh | B2 | 67 | Koup | E1 | 61 | Leipoldtville | C4 | 62 | Machadodorp | B5 | 81 |
| Kingscote | D2 | 66 | Koutjie | A5 | 60 | Lekfontein | F5 | 65 | Macleantown | B5 | 66 |
| Kingsley | A3 | 75 | Kraaifontein | B2 | 60 | Lekkersing | B5 | 68 | Maclear | C3 | 66 |
| Kingswood | E3 | 71 | Kraaldorings | E1 | 61 | Lemoenshoek | D2 | 60 | Madadeni | A3 | 75 |
| Kinirapoort | C2 | 66 | Kraankuil | C1 | 65 | Lephalale | C2 | 79 | Madibogo | D1 | 71 |
| Kinross | C1 | 73 | Kransfontein | C4 | 73 | Letjiesbos | A5 | 64 | Madipelesa | C3 | 71 |
| Kirkwood | D4 | 60 | Kranskop | A5 | 75 | Letsitele | B3 | 81 | Mafeteng | B1 | 66 |
| Klaarstroom | A4 | 60 | Kriel | C1 | 73 | Leydsdorp | B3 | 81 | Mafikeng | H5 | 77 |
| Klaserie | C4 | 81 | Kromdraai | A5 | 81 | Libertas | B4 | 73 | Mafube | D2 | 66 |
| Klawer | C4 | 62 | Kroonstad | A3 | 73 | Libode | D3 | 66 | Magaliesburg | A1 | 73 |
| Klein Drakenstein | B2 | 60 | Krugers | E1 | 65 | Lichtenburg | E1 | 71 | Magudu | C3 | 75 |
| Klein Letaba | B2 | 81 | Krugersdorp | B1 | 73 | Lidgetton | A1 | 67 | Mahlabatini | B4 | 75 |
| Klein Tswaing | C2 | 71 | Kruidfontein | G5 | 63 | Limburg | D3 | 79 | Mahlangasi | C3 | 75 |
| Kleinbegin | C4 | 69 | Kruisfontein | D5 | 60 | Lime Acres | B4 | 70 | Mahwelereng | D3 | 79 |
| Kleinmond | B3 | 60 | Kruisrivier | E1 | 61 | Lindeshof | C2 | 60 | Maizefield | D2 | 73 |
| Kleinpoort | D4 | 60 | Kuboes | B4 | 68 | Lindley | B3 | 73 | Makwassie | E2 | 71 |
| Kleinsee | A1 | 62 | Kuilsriver | B2 | 60 | Llandudno | B2 | 60 | Malaita | A4 | 81 |
| Klerksdorp | F2 | 71 | Ku-Mayima | C3 | 66 | Loch Vaal | B2 | 73 | Maleoskop | A4 | 81 |
| Klerkskraal | A1 | 73 | Kuruman | B3 | 70 | Lochiel | B1 | 75 | Malgas | D3 | 60 |
| Klipdale | C3 | 60 | KwaDweshula | A2 | 67 | Loerie | D5 | 60 | Malmesbury | B2 | 60 |
| Klipfontein | D1 | 73 | KwaDukuza | | | Loeriesfontein | D3 | 63 | Mamaila | B2 | 81 |
| Klipplaat | C5 | 65 | (Stanger) | C1 | 67 | Lofter | E2 | 65 | Mamre | B2 | 60 |
| Kliprand | C2 | 62 | Kwaggaskop | B5 | 81 | Logageng | G5 | 77 | Mandini | B5 | 75 |
| Klipspruit | B5 | 81 | KwaMashu | B1 | 67 | Lohatlha | A3 | 70 | Mangeni | A4 | 75 |
| Knapdaar | F2 | 65 | KwaMbonambi | C4 | 75 | Long Hope | E5 | 65 | Manthestad | D3 | 71 |
| Knysna | B5 | 60 | Kwamhlanga | D5 | 79 | Loskop | D5 | 73 | Mantsonyane | C1 | 66 |
| Koedoeskop | B4 | 79 | Kylemore | B2 | 60 | Lothair | A1 | 75 | Mapumulo | B5 | 75 |
| Koegas | D5 | 69 | Laaiplek | A1 | 60 | Louis Trichardt | | | Marakabei | C1 | 66 |
| Koegrabie | C5 | 69 | Labera | F5 | 77 | (Makhado) | B2 | 81 | Marble Hall | A4 | 81 |

| Name | Grid | Pg | Name | Grid | Pg | Name | Grid | Pg | Name | Grid | Pg |
|---|---|---|---|---|---|---|---|---|---|---|---|
| Marburg | A3 | 67 | Millvale | B5 | 79 | Mpumalanga | B1 | 67 | Nkwalini | B4 | 75 |
| Marchand | B4 | 69 | Milnerton | B2 | 60 | Mt Moorosi | C2 | 66 | Nobantu | D3 | 66 |
| Margate | A3 | 67 | Mirage | F2 | 71 | Mthatha | D3 | 66 | Nobhokhwe | B4 | 66 |
| Maricosdraai | A3 | 79 | Misgund | B5 | 60 | Mtkonjeneni | B4 | 75 | Noenieput | A3 | 69 |
| Marikana | B5 | 79 | Mkambati | A3 | 67 | Mtubatuba | C4 | 75 | Noll | B5 | 60 |
| Marite | C4 | 81 | Mkuze | C3 | 75 | Mtunzini | C5 | 75 | Nondweni | A4 | 75 |
| Marken | D2 | 79 | Mmabatho | H5 | 77 | Mtwalume | B2 | 67 | Nongoma | B3 | 75 |
| Marnitz | C2 | 79 | Modderrivier | C5 | 71 | Muden | A5 | 75 | Noordhoek | B2 | 60 |
| Marquard | A4 | 73 | Modimolle | C4 | 79 | Muizenberg | B2 | 60 | Noordkaap | C5 | 81 |
| Martin's Drift | C2 | 79 | Modjadjiskloof | B3 | 81 | Munster | A3 | 67 | Noordkuil | C5 | 62 |
| Marydale | D5 | 69 | Moeswal | D3 | 69 | Munyu | C4 | 66 | Normandien | D3 | 73 |
| Mashashane | A3 | 81 | Mogalakwena | D3 | 79 | Murchison | C3 | 81 | Northam | B4 | 79 |
| Masisi | C1 | 81 | Mogwadi | A2 | 81 | Murraysburg | C4 | 65 | Norvalspont | E2 | 65 |
| Matatiele | D2 | 66 | Mogwase | B4 | 79 | Musina | B1 | 81 | Nottingham Road | D5 | 73 |
| Matavhelo | C1 | 81 | Mohales Hoek | B2 | 66 | Mynfontein | C3 | 65 | Noupoort | D3 | 65 |
| Matjiesfontein | D1 | 60 | Mokamole | D3 | 79 | Nababeep | B1 | 62 | Nqabarha | D4 | 66 |
| Matjiesrivier | A4 | 60 | Mokopane | D3 | 79 | Nabies | A4 | 69 | Nqutu | A4 | 75 |
| Matlabas | B3 | 79 | Moloporivier | F5 | 77 | Nakop | A3 | 69 | Ntabamhlope | D5 | 73 |
| Matlala | A3 | 81 | Molteno | F3 | 65 | Namakgale | C3 | 81 | Ntabankulu | D3 | 66 |
| Matroosberg | C1 | 60 | Mont Pelaan | D3 | 73 | Namies | D5 | 68 | Ntibane | C3 | 66 |
| Mavamba | C2 | 81 | Montagu | D2 | 60 | Napier | C3 | 60 | Ntseshe | C4 | 66 |
| Mazenod | B1 | 66 | Monte Christo | C2 | 79 | Nariep | B3 | 62 | Ntshilini | D4 | 66 |
| Mazeppa Bay | C5 | 66 | Mooi River | D5 | 73 | Nature's Valley | B5 | 60 | Ntywenka | C3 | 66 |
| Mbashe Bridge | C4 | 66 | Mooifontein | E1 | 71 | Ncanara | E5 | 61 | Nutfield | D4 | 79 |
| Mbazwana | D3 | 75 | Mooketsi | B2 | 81 | Ndumo | C2 | 75 | Nuwerus | C3 | 62 |
| Mbotyi | A3 | 67 | Mookgophong | D4 | 79 | Ndundulu | B4 | 75 | Nuy | C2 | 60 |
| McGregor | C2 | 60 | Moordkuil | C2 | 60 | Ndwedwe | B1 | 67 | Nyokana | C4 | 66 |
| Mdantsane | G4 | 61 | Moorreesburg | B1 | 60 | Neilersdrif | C4 | 69 | Oatlands | C5 | 65 |
| Meadows | A1 | 66 | Mopane | B1 | 81 | Nelspoort | B4 | 64 | Obobogorap | A2 | 69 |
| Melkbosstrand | B2 | 60 | Morebeng | B2 | 81 | Nelspruit | C5 | 81 | Odendaalsrus | F3 | 71 |
| Melmoth | B4 | 75 | Morgan's Bay | C5 | 66 | New Amalfi | D2 | 66 | Ofcolaco | B3 | 81 |
| Meltonwold | A3 | 64 | Morgenzon | D2 | 73 | New England | B3 | 66 | Ogies | C1 | 73 |
| Memel | D3 | 73 | Morokweng | A2 | 70 | New Hanover | B1 | 67 | Ohrigstad | B4 | 81 |
| Merindol | F1 | 71 | Morristown | B3 | 66 | New Machavie | F2 | 71 | Okiep | B1 | 62 |
| Merriman | C3 | 65 | Mortimer | E4 | 65 | Newcastle | D3 | 73 | Old Bunting | D4 | 66 |
| Merweville | G5 | 63 | Moshesh's Ford | B3 | 66 | Ngcobo | C4 | 66 | Old Morley | D4 | 66 |
| Mesa | F1 | 71 | Mosita | D1 | 71 | Ngobeni | B3 | 75 | Olifantshoek | A3 | 70 |
| Mesklip | B1 | 62 | Mossel Bay | A5 | 60 | Ngome | B3 | 75 | Olyfberg | B3 | 81 |
| Meyerton | B2 | 73 | Mossiesdal | A5 | 81 | Ngqamakhwe | C4 | 66 | Omdraaisvlei | B2 | 64 |
| Meyerville | C2 | 73 | Motetema | A4 | 81 | Ngqeleni | D4 | 66 | Onderstedorings | F2 | 63 |
| Mgwali | B5 | 66 | Mothibistad | B2 | 70 | Ngqungqu | C4 | 66 | Ons Hoop | C2 | 79 |
| Mica | C3 | 81 | Mount Ayliff | D3 | 66 | Niekerkshoop | A5 | 70 | Ontmoeting | C2 | 69 |
| Middelburg | A5 | 81 | Mount Fletcher | C2 | 66 | Nietverdiend | A4 | 79 | Oorwinning | B2 | 81 |
| Middelburg | D3 | 65 | Mount Frere | D3 | 66 | Nieu-Bethesda | D4 | 65 | Oostermoed | B4 | 79 |
| Middelfontein | D4 | 79 | Mount Rupert | C3 | 71 | Nieuwoudtville | D3 | 63 | Orania | D1 | 65 |
| Middelpos | E4 | 63 | Mount Stewart | D5 | 65 | Nigel | C1 | 73 | Oranjefontein | C2 | 79 |
| Middelwit | B4 | 79 | Moyeni | B2 | 66 | Nigramoep | B5 | 68 | Oranjerivier | C5 | 71 |
| Middleton | E5 | 65 | Mpemvana | A3 | 75 | Nkambak | B3 | 81 | Oranjeville | B2 | 73 |
| Midrand | B1 | 73 | Mpethu | C5 | 66 | Nkandla | B4 | 75 | Orkney | F2 | 71 |
| Migdol | D2 | 71 | Mphaki | C2 | 66 | Nkau | C2 | 66 | Osborn | B4 | 75 |
| Miller | C5 | 65 | Mpolweni | A5 | 75 | Nkomo | C2 | 81 | oSizweni | A3 | 75 |

| Name | Grid | No. | Name | Grid | No. | Name | Grid | No. | Name | Grid | No. |
|---|---|---|---|---|---|---|---|---|---|---|---|
| Ottosdal | E2 | 71 | Pietermaritzburg | B1 | 67 | Qoqodala | F4 | 65 | Roedtan | A4 | 81 |
| Oudtshoorn | A4 | 60 | Piketberg | D5 | 63 | Qudeni | A4 | 75 | Roma | B1 | 66 |
| Oukraal | C3 | 60 | Pilgrim's Rest | C4 | 81 | Queensburgh | B2 | 67 | Rondevlei | A5 | 60 |
| Ouplaas | D3 | 60 | Pinetown | B1 | 67 | Queenstown | F4 | 65 | Roodebank | C2 | 73 |
| Oviston | E2 | 65 | Platbakkies | C2 | 62 | Quko | C5 | 66 | Roodepoort | B1 | 73 |
| Owendale | B4 | 70 | Plathuis | D2 | 60 | Qumbu | D3 | 66 | Rooiberg | C4 | 79 |
| Oyster Bay | D5 | 60 | Platrand | D2 | 73 | Radium | C4 | 79 | Rooibokkraal | B3 | 79 |
| Paarl | B2 | 60 | Plettenberg Bay | B5 | 60 | Ramabanta | B1 | 66 | Rooibosbult | B3 | 79 |
| Pacaltsdorp | A5 | 60 | Plooysburg | C5 | 71 | Ramatlabama | H5 | 77 | Rooigrond | H5 | 77 |
| Paddock | A3 | 67 | Pniel | B2 | 60 | Ramsgate | A3 | 67 | Rooikraal | A5 | 81 |
| Pafuri | D1 | 81 | Pofadder | A5 | 69 | Randalhurst | B4 | 75 | Rooipan | C5 | 71 |
| Palala | D3 | 79 | Politsi | B3 | 81 | Randburg | B1 | 73 | Rooiwal | A2 | 73 |
| Paleisheuwel | D5 | 63 | Polokwane | A3 | 81 | Randfontein | B1 | 73 | Roosboom | D4 | 73 |
| Palmerton | D3 | 66 | Pomeroy | A4 | 75 | Ratelfontein | C4 | 62 | Roossenekal | B4 | 81 |
| Palmietfontein | B2 | 66 | Pongola | C3 | 75 | Rawsonville | C2 | 60 | Rorke's Drift | A4 | 75 |
| Pampierstad | C3 | 71 | Pools | D5 | 63 | Rayton | D5 | 79 | Rosebank | A2 | 67 |
| Pampoenpoort | A3 | 64 | Port Alfred | F5 | 61 | Redcliffe | D5 | 73 | Rosedene | A4 | 64 |
| Panbult | A2 | 75 | Port Beaufort | D3 | 60 | Reddersburg | F1 | 65 | Rosendal | B4 | 73 |
| Pansdrif | C5 | 79 | Port Edward | A3 | 67 | Redelinghuys | C5 | 62 | Rosetta | D5 | 73 |
| Papendorp | C4 | 62 | Port Elizabeth | E5 | 61 | Redoubt | A3 | 67 | Rosmead | D3 | 65 |
| Papiesvlei | C3 | 60 | Port Grosvenor | A3 | 67 | Reebokrand | D1 | 65 | Rossouw | B3 | 66 |
| Papkuil | B4 | 70 | Port Nolloth | B5 | 68 | Reitz | B3 | 73 | Rostrataville | E2 | 71 |
| Park Rynie | B2 | 67 | Port Shepstone | B3 | 67 | Reitzburg | A2 | 73 | Rouxpos | E1 | 61 |
| Parow | B2 | 60 | Port St Johns | D4 | 66 | Reivilo | C3 | 71 | Rouxville | A2 | 66 |
| Parys | A2 | 73 | Porterville | D5 | 63 | Renosterkop | B4 | 64 | Ruitersbos | E2 | 61 |
| Patensie | D5 | 60 | Post Chalmers | E4 | 65 | Renosterspruit | F2 | 71 | Rust de Winter | D4 | 79 |
| Paternoster | B5 | 62 | Postmasburg | A4 | 70 | Restvale | B4 | 64 | Rust | B1 | 60 |
| Paterson | E4 | 61 | Potchefstroom | | | Rhodes | C2 | 66 | Rustenburg | B5 | 79 |
| Paul Roux | B4 | 73 | (Tlokwe) | A2 | 73 | Richards Bay | C5 | 75 | Rustig | F3 | 71 |
| Paulpietersburg | B3 | 75 | Potfontein | C2 | 65 | Richmond | C3 | 65 | Rusverby | A5 | 79 |
| Pearly Beach | C3 | 60 | Potsdam | G4 | 61 | Riebeeckstad | F3 | 71 | Saaifontein | G4 | 63 |
| Pearston | D5 | 65 | Poupan | C1 | 65 | Riebeek Kasteel | B1 | 60 | Sabie | C4 | 81 |
| Peddie | F4 | 61 | Pretoria | C5 | 79 | Riebeek East | E4 | 61 | Sada | F4 | 65 |
| Pella | D5 | 68 | Prieska | A5 | 70 | Riebeek-Wes | B1 | 60 | Sakrivier | E3 | 63 |
| Penge | B3 | 81 | Prince Albert | E1 | 61 | Rietbron | B5 | 64 | Saldanha | A1 | 60 |
| Perdekop | D2 | 73 | Prince Albert | | | Rietfontein | A2 | 69 | Salem | F4 | 61 |
| Petersburg | D4 | 65 | Road | G5 | 63 | Rietkuil | C3 | 73 | Salpeterpan | C2 | 71 |
| Petrus Steyn | B3 | 73 | Prince Alfred | | | Rietpoel | C3 | 60 | Salt Lake | C5 | 71 |
| Petrusburg | D5 | 71 | Hamlet | C1 | 60 | Rietpoort | B3 | 62 | Salt Rock | C1 | 67 |
| Petrusville | D1 | 65 | Pringle Bay | B3 | 60 | Rietvlei | A5 | 75 | Sand River Valley | D4 | 73 |
| Phalaborwa | C3 | 81 | Priors | E2 | 65 | Rita | A3 | 81 | Sandberg | C4 | 62 |
| Philadelphia | B2 | 60 | Protem | D3 | 60 | Ritchie | C5 | 71 | Sandton | B1 | 73 |
| Philippolis | E2 | 65 | Pudimoe | C3 | 71 | River View | C4 | 75 | Sandvlakte | C5 | 60 |
| Philippolis Road | E2 | 65 | Puntjie | E3 | 61 | Riversdale | E2 | 61 | Sannaspos | F5 | 71 |
| Philipstown | D2 | 65 | Putsonderwater | D5 | 69 | Riverside | A2 | 67 | Sannieshof | E1 | 71 |
| Phokwane | A4 | 81 | Qacha's Nek | D2 | 66 | Riviersonderend | C2 | 60 | Sasolburg | B2 | 73 |
| Phuthaditjhaba | C4 | 73 | Qamata | B4 | 66 | Roamer's Rest | C2 | 66 | Sauer | C5 | 62 |
| Pienaarsrivier | C4 | 79 | Qholhora Mouth | C5 | 66 | Robert's Drift | C2 | 73 | Scarborough | B2 | 60 |
| Piet Plessis | C1 | 71 | Qhorha Mouth | C5 | 66 | Robertson | C2 | 60 | Scheepersnek | A3 | 75 |
| Piet Retief | B2 | 75 | Qiba | B3 | 66 | Rode | D3 | 66 | Schmidtsdrif | C4 | 71 |
| Pieter Meintjies | D1 | 60 | Qoboqobo | C5 | 66 | Rodenbeck | E5 | 71 | Schoombee | E3 | 65 |

| Name | Grid | Pg | Name | Grid | Pg | Name | Grid | Pg | Name | Grid | Pg |
|---|---|---|---|---|---|---|---|---|---|---|---|
| Schweizer-Reneke | D2 | 71 | Somerset West | B2 | 60 | Straatsdrif | A4 | 79 | Three Sisters | B4 | 64 |
| Scottburgh | B2 | 67 | Somkele | C4 | 75 | Strand | B2 | 60 | Tierfontein | E3 | 71 |
| Sea Park | B3 | 67 | Sonstraal | D2 | 69 | Strandfontein | C4 | 62 | Tierpoort | F1 | 65 |
| Sea View | D5 | 60 | Southbroom | A3 | 67 | Struisbaai | D3 | 60 | Tina Bridge | D3 | 66 |
| Secunda | C2 | 73 | Southeyville | B4 | 66 | Strydenburg | C1 | 65 | Tinmyne | D3 | 79 |
| Sedgefield | B5 | 60 | Southwell | F5 | 61 | Strydpoort | E2 | 71 | Tolwe | D2 | 79 |
| Seekoegat | A5 | 64 | Soutpan | C5 | 79 | Studtis | C4 | 60 | Tom Burke | C2 | 79 |
| Sekhukhune | B4 | 81 | Soweto | B1 | 73 | Stutterheim | B5 | 66 | Tombo | D4 | 66 |
| Selonsrivier | A5 | 81 | Spanwerk | B3 | 79 | Summerstrand | E5 | 61 | Tompi Seleka | A4 | 81 |
| Sendelingsdrif | A4 | 68 | Spes Bona | A2 | 73 | Sun City/ Lost City | B5 | 79 | Tonash | D1 | 79 |
| Senekal | A4 | 73 | Spitskopvlei | D4 | 65 | Sunland | E4 | 61 | Tongaat | B1 | 67 |
| Senlac | E5 | 77 | Spoegrivier | B2 | 62 | Sutherland | F4 | 63 | Tontelbos | E3 | 63 |
| Sentrum | B3 | 79 | Spring Valley | F4 | 65 | Sutton | A3 | 70 | Tosca | F5 | 77 |
| Senwabarana | A2 | 81 | Springbok | B1 | 62 | Suurbraak | D2 | 60 | Touws River | C1 | 60 |
| Seringkop | D5 | 79 | Springfontein | E2 | 65 | Swaershoek | E5 | 65 | Trawal | C4 | 62 |
| Seshego | A3 | 81 | Springs | C1 | 73 | Swartberg | D2 | 66 | Trichardt | C2 | 73 |
| Setlagole | D1 | 71 | Spytfontein | C4 | 71 | Swartkops | E5 | 61 | Trichardtsdal | B3 | 81 |
| Settlers | D4 | 79 | St Faith's | A2 | 67 | Swartmodder | B3 | 69 | Triple Streams | C3 | 66 |
| Sevenoaks | A5 | 75 | St Francis Bay | D5 | 60 | Swartplaas | A1 | 73 | Trompsburg | E1 | 65 |
| Severn | A2 | 70 | St Helena Bay | C5 | 62 | Swartputs | B4 | 70 | Tsazo | C4 | 66 |
| Seweweekspoort | E1 | 61 | St Lucia | C4 | 75 | Swartruggens | A5 | 79 | Tshakhuma | B2 | 81 |
| Seymour | F5 | 65 | St Marks | B4 | 66 | Swartwater | C1 | 79 | Tshani | D4 | 66 |
| Sezela | B2 | 67 | Staansaam | B2 | 69 | Swellendam | D2 | 60 | Tshipise | B1 | 81 |
| Shaka's Rock | C1 | 67 | Stafford's Post | A2 | 67 | Swempoort | B3 | 66 | Tsineng | A2 | 70 |
| Shakaskraal | C1 | 67 | Standerton | C2 | 73 | Swinburne | C4 | 73 | Tsitsa Bridge | D3 | 66 |
| Shannon | E5 | 71 | Stanford | C3 | 60 | Syfergat | A3 | 66 | Tsoelike | D2 | 66 |
| Sheepmoor | A2 | 75 | Steekdorings | C2 | 71 | Tafelberg | D3 | 65 | Tsolo | D3 | 66 |
| Sheldon | E5 | 65 | Steelpoort | B4 | 81 | Tainton | C5 | 66 | Tsomo | B4 | 66 |
| Sherborne | D3 | 65 | Steilloopbrug | D2 | 79 | Taleni | C4 | 66 | Tugela Ferry | A4 | 75 |
| Sidwadweni | D3 | 66 | Steilrand | B3 | 75 | Tarkastad | F4 | 65 | Tugela Mouth | B5 | 75 |
| Sigoga | D2 | 66 | Steinkopf | C5 | 68 | Taung | D3 | 71 | Tuinplaas | D4 | 79 |
| Silkaatskop | A4 | 79 | Stella | D1 | 71 | Temba | C5 | 79 | Tulbagh | C1 | 60 |
| Silutshana | A4 | 75 | Stellenbosch | B2 | 60 | Tembisa | B1 | 73 | Tunnel | C1 | 60 |
| Silver Streams | B4 | 70 | Sterkaar | C3 | 65 | Terra Firma | E5 | 77 | Tweefontein | E4 | 63 |
| Simon's Town | B3 | 60 | Sterkspruit | B2 | 66 | Teviot | E4 | 65 | Tweeling | C3 | 73 |
| Sinksabrug | A5 | 60 | Sterkstroom | F3 | 65 | Teza | C4 | 75 | Tweespruit | F5 | 71 |
| Sir Lowry's Pass | B2 | 60 | Sterling | G3 | 63 | Thaba Chitja | C2 | 66 | Tyira | D3 | 66 |
| Sishen | A3 | 70 | Steynsburg | E3 | 65 | Thaba 'Nchu | F5 | 71 | Tylden | B4 | 66 |
| Sittingbourne | B5 | 66 | Steynsrus | A3 | 73 | Thaba Tseka | C1 | 66 | Tzaneen | B3 | 81 |
| Siyabuswa | A4 | 81 | Steytlerville | C4 | 60 | Thabazimbi | B4 | 79 | Ubombo | C3 | 75 |
| Skeerpoort | C5 | 79 | Stilfontein | F2 | 71 | The Crags | B5 | 60 | Ugie | C3 | 66 |
| Skipskop | D3 | 60 | Still Bay East | E3 | 61 | The Downs | B3 | 81 | Uitenhage | D5 | 60 |
| Skuinsdrif | A5 | 79 | Still Bay West | E3 | 61 | The Haven | D4 | 66 | Uitkyk | C1 | 62 |
| Slurry | H5 | 77 | Stockpoort | B2 | 79 | The Heads | B5 | 60 | Uitspankraal | D4 | 63 |
| Smithfield | A2 | 66 | Stoffberg | B5 | 81 | The Ranch | A5 | 75 | Ulco | C4 | 71 |
| Smitskraal | C5 | 60 | Stofvlei | C2 | 62 | Theron | F4 | 71 | uLundi | B4 | 75 |
| Sneeukraal | A4 | 64 | Stompneusbaai | B5 | 62 | Theunissen | F4 | 71 | uMbogintwini | B2 | 67 |
| Sodium | B2 | 64 | Stoneyridge | D3 | 66 | Thohoyandou | C2 | 81 | uMgababa | B2 | 67 |
| Soebatsfontein | B2 | 62 | Stormberg | F3 | 65 | Thorndale | A2 | 81 | uMhlanga | B1 | 67 |
| Somerset East | E5 | 65 | Stormsrivier | C5 | 60 | Thornville | B1 | 67 | uMkomaas | B2 | 67 |
|  |  |  | Stormsvlei | D2 | 60 |  |  |  | uMlazi | B2 | 67 |